STANDARD LOAN

UNLESS RECALLED BY ANOTHER READER
THIS ITEM MAY BE BORROWED FOR

FOUR WEEKS

Questions Literacy Resources

Bill's New Frock

Compiled by Marian Dean

Activities and teachers' notes based on the novel by Anne Fine

THE QUESTIONS PUBLISHING COMPANY LTD
BIRMINGHAM
2000

First published in 2000 by
The Questions Publishing Company Ltd
27 Frederick Street, Birmingham B1 3HH

Designed by Al Stewart
Edited by Audrey Bamber
Cover design by John Minnett

ISBN: 1-84190-030-3

Also available from the The Questions Publishing Company Ltd:

Questions Literacy Resources: *The Story of Tracy Beaker*
compiled by Liz Ross, from the novel by Jacqueline Wilson

Contents

Introduction

How to use this resource

Bill's New Frock tells us of Bill's Kafkaesque experiences as he wakes to find that he is a girl. Not only does he discover he is a girl but everybody he meets during his day treats him as though he has never been anything other than a girl. Through Bill, Anne Fine suggests that the ways in which life is different for boys and girls and the issues raised are all ones which pupils can recognise, and perhaps identify with and almost certainly have opinions on.

This resource pack is presented in two parts:

Part I is for planning literacy hours for the key stage 2 classroom. The strategies and tasks will be linked to a fifteen-minute reading. *Bill's New Frock* has seven chapters, and in order to fit it into a four- or five-day week of literacy hours some chapters could be selected for the literacy hours, and the remaining chapters could be read to pupils at other times, following straight on from the chapter which is to be used for teaching purposes, either through private reading or by listening to an audio tape. Chivers Audio Books of Windsor Bridge Road, Bath BA2 3AX has produced an audio tape pack of Tony Robinson reading *Bill's New Frock* along with *The Country Pancake*, also by Anne Fine.

At the beginning of each chapter I have included a chart outlining characters, events and settings with a fourth column headed comments. I found it useful to note down ideas, chapter by chapter as I read the book, then use those notes to generate initial ideas, linking the text to the literacy strategy. Some of the ideas in the comments column have become teaching ideas and others have not. This column may prove useful to you in devising further ways of using *Bill's New Frock* in your classroom.

This resource is based on a week of literacy hours taught in year 6, term 2. The text, sentence and word level work is linked closely to that year and term in order to maintain links between the tasks, the text and other, related texts. It is also possible to adapt the pack for use in other years and terms.

The ways in which the text can be used for the literacy hour are listed, chapter by chapter, under the following headings:

- Whole class work: shared text (including suggested discussion points for during or after the reading).
- Whole class work: sentence and word level.
- Guided reading/writing: teacher-led tasks. These tasks have been differentiated into three levels, starting with a generic version, labelled A followed by a supported task, labelled B and then an extension task C.
- Independent group work: These tasks are linked to chapters but can be used on a carousel basis. Some of the tasks can be introduced later in a series of literacy hours. These are also labelled generic A, supported B, extension C. Pupils can either do the tasks you consider to be at the most appropriate level or move through the levels. For convenience and clarity, many of these tasks are presented in the form of work-sheets. However, I do not wish to give the impression that all group work should be in this form. Many of the tasks could be completed in an exercise book, a file, a display format, or on the computer.
- Plenary sessions

I have quoted short extracts of text which will need preparing beforehand, by placing on to overhead transparency (OHT), whiteboard, flip-chart and so on, for sharing with the whole class. For longer extracts, I have quoted the page and paragraph number from the 1990 edition, published by Mammoth Books: ISBN 0-7497-0305-9.

Part II suggests ways in which *Bill's New Frock* can be used to support and develop literacy or teaching in other subject areas beyond the literacy hour. These can be used with pupils who have read the whole book. You could also use them if you have taken a more flexible approach to the literacy hour, for example, in terms of how many days a week it is delivered. Some of the tasks could also be incorporated into literacy hours.

National Literacy Strategy main focus areas

Word level

Identify mis-spelt words	Y6T2	1
Investigate meanings and spellings of connectives	Y6T1	6
Using dictionaries	Y6T2	3
Word origins and derivations	Y6T2	5
Proverbs	Y6T2	6

Sentence level

Sentence construction and punctuation, particularly compound and complex sentences	Y6T2	3
Contracting sentences for summarising	Y6T2	4
Use of conditional forms	Y6T2	5

Text level

Reading comprehension		
Aspects of narrative structure (time)	Y6T2	1
Structure of paragraphs	Y6T2	2
Success of texts in evoking feelings	Y6T2	8

Writing composition

Different genres (genre swapping)	Y6T2	10
Alternative endings	Y6T2	10
Commentary/summary	Y6T2	14

National Literacy Strategy
secondary focus areas
(These are listed only when they are first cited.)

Word level

Building from other words with similar patterns and meanings	Y3T1	6
Common prefixes	Y3T1	10
Recognise common letter strings	Y3T3	6
Identify short words within longer words	Y3T3	8
Collection of synonyms	Y3T3	13
Use of dictionaries to provide further information about words	Y3T3	15
Formation of diminutives	Y4T3	12
Building up words by syllabic parts	Y5T2	3

Sentence level

How sentences can be joined in more complex ways	Y3T3	5
Recognise how commas, connectives, full stops join and separate clauses	Y4T2	4
Use of connectives	Y4T3	4
Investigate clauses	Y5T3	6
Connectives	Y5T3	7
Construction of complex sentences	Y6T1	1

Text level

Different voices	Y3T1	3
Generating ideas for writing	Y3T1	9
Discuss, evaluate characters	Y3T2	3
Discuss characters' feelings, behaviour, etc.	Y3T3	5
Explore chronology in narrative	Y4T1	3
Poetry writing	Y4T1	14
Settings and incidents	Y4T2	2
Notemaking	Y4T2	14
Dilemmas in stories	Y4T3	1
Write critically about a dilemma	Y4T3	8
Alternative endings	Y4T3	12
Poems of different styles and structures	Y4T3	14
Summarising	Y6T1	8

National Curriculum links:
English at Key Stage 2 Programmes of Study

Speaking and Listening

Range:
  1a Talking for a range of purposes
  1c Listening, responding and commenting

Key skills:
  2a Confident and clear expression
      Opportunities to make a range of contributions in discussion
  2b Listening to others and identifying key points in a discussion

Standard English and language study:
  3b Discussion of more imaginative and adventurous choices of words

Reading

Range:
  1a Pupils should become enthusiastic, independent and reflective readers

Independent and shared reading:
  1c Use of texts with challenging subject matter
  1d Modern fiction of significant children's authors

Key skills:
  2a Increase ability to read with fluency, understanding and enjoyment
  2b Pupils should respond imaginatively to plot, characters, ideas, vocabulary and organisation of the text
      Evaluation of the text

Standard English and language study:
  3 Use of terms: author, setting, plot, format
     Develop understanding of the structure, vocabulary and grammar of standard English

Writing

Range:
    1a Write for varied purposes
    1c Use the characteristics of different writing

Key skills:
    2b Opportunities to plan and draft
    2d Use of dictionaries

Standard English and language study:
    3b Develop the understanding of the grammar of complex sentences
    3b Use of paragraphs

Part I

Using Bill's New Frock *in the Literacy Hour*

Chapter 1

A Really Awful Start

Characters	Settings	Events	Comments
Bill Simpson	Home	Bill becomes a girl	
Mother	Route to school	Dresses Bill in pink frock	
Father		Calls him poppet	
Bella the cat		Behaves as always	
Mean Malcolm & the gang of boys		Whistle at him	
Elderly woman		Takes him across the road	
Headmaster	School	Although he is as late as the boys, he is not told off	
Mrs Collins	School assembly	Is told off for fiddling with his dress – feels exposed. Boys are picked to carry a table.	
Astrid		Complains that only boys are chosen to carry things	A minor character who makes an important point
Flora, Kirsty, Nick, Philip and Talilah	Classroom		None of them is wearing a frock
	Classroom	Handwriting lesson	Bill writes more neatly than usual but is told off. Philip's writing is a mess but he is praised for his effort
		Rapunzel	Bill questions Rapunzel's role

Whole-class shared text work

Focus areas for discussion

- The attitudes and behaviour of Bill's father and the headmaster.
- The issue of the different expectations of Bill's handwriting; an introduction to gender issues.
- An awareness of narrative time compared to reading time.
- Prediction based on the notion that a story could have taken different directions.

Text level: attitudes and behaviour

The two extracts highlighted below inform us how Bill is going to be treated as the day goes on. One of the ways in which Anne Fine maintains the idea of Bill as a girl, is that no one addresses him by name. If you begin with the questions I have listed under the extract, there are then opportunities to discuss the use of 'poppet' and 'dear' by the author, as well as the characters:

Mr Simpson leaned over and planted a kiss on Bill's cheek.
'Bye, Poppet,' he said, ruffling Bill's curls. 'You look very sweet today. It's not often we see you in a frock, is it?' (pp. 9–10)

1. Is this the way Mr Simpson would normally address his son?
2. Why does Mr Simpson call him 'poppet' rather than Bill?

'Late, Andrew!' the headmaster called out fiercely. 'Late, late, late!'
Then it was Bill's turn to go past.
'That's right,' the headmaster called encouragingly. 'Hurry along dear. We don't want to miss assembly, do we?' (p. 12)

1. Did Bill expect to be addressed in the way he was by the head?
2. Why did the head call him 'dear' rather than Bill?

Text level: introduction to gender issues

The extract from page 16, paragraph 2 to page 18, end of paragraph 2: 'He wrote more than . . . Keep up the good work', is very useful to prepare in advance. Not only does it introduce the way in which the day is going to be very different for Bill in graphic terms when his handwriting is not considered neat enough, it also presents an excellent opportunity for sentence-level work on similes. So the main questions to ask are:

1. Why was Mrs Collins so critical of Bill's writing but approved of Philip's?
2. How did Bill feel when Mrs Collins told him off about his writing?

Whole-class work

Sentence level: sentence structure

Simple, compound and complex sentences
The chart lists some examples of simple, compound and complex sentences from the text. Anne Fine often starts her sentences with *and*, *so* or *but* and because of that it may seem initially that they do not to fit the definitions of simple, compound or complex. However, after careful reading of several grammar books, a case can be made for using all the selected sentences in the exercise below and subsequent exercises. Although I have not focused on the aspect of sentences that start with *and*, many pupils and adults share the belief that starting a sentence with *and* is incorrect. Usually this belief stems from teaching which intends to extend the range of conjunctions used by young writers. It is an interesting area to explore, particularly with a writer who clearly does not mind starting sentences with *and*, *but* or *so*. Later tasks address this aspect of the book.

Simple sentences	Compound sentences	Complex sentences
She meant him.	So Bill picked up his pen and opened his books.	Some of the letters were so enormous they looked like giants herding the small letters haphazardly across the page.
He knew it.		

(pp. 16–17)

Simile
Some of the letters were so _____ they looked like _____ _____ the small letters haphazardly across the page.

This complex sentence can be used to introduce or revise similes. Pupils can offer suggestions of their own, but if they find it difficult, use the word level activity below.

Word level: vocabulary development

If pupils find it difficult to construct their own similes, the vocabulary below may support them in this task. In addition, further work may be undertaken in identifying *synonyms, antonyms, word origins, adverbs* and *adjectives*, and *common letter strings*. An expanded list would provide opportunities to identify prefixes and suffixes.

enormous
huge
gigantic
massive
immense
colossal
vast
gargantuan
mammoth
tremendous
stupendous

tiny
minute
minuscule
microscopic
miniature
diminutive
small
little
Lilliputian

haphazardly
carelessly
disorderly
in a disorganised way
in a slipshod way
in a slapdash way

Word level: spelling – the meaning of 'min-'

Using the words from the formation of similes, pupils can explore words containing or starting with 'min-' and link these to the meaning 'small':

1. Identify relevant words from the vocabulary list for the similes task.
2. Add words or phrases suggested by pupil (*minim, mini skirt, mini car, diminish*).
3. Discuss 'min-' or 'mini-' related to small:
    minute
    minuscule
    miniature
    diminutive
4. Give pupils cards (see below).
5. Pupils can line up at the front of the class to reassemble these and any other words you would like to include.
6. Extend the list beyond words relating to small (mint, minus).
7. Use different dictionaries to discover the origin of 'min-' or 'mini-'.
8. Use the terms *prefix* (di-) and *suffix* (-ive).

di   min   ut   ive   ute   iature

(Several 'min' cards will be needed.)

Word/sentence level: punctuation

Using a related text
The poem *According to my Mood* by Benjamin Zephaniah is ideal for whole class teaching and exploring punctuation and aspects of handwriting. The first two lines are:

I have poetic licence, i WriTe thE way i waNt.
i drop my full stops where i like . . .
(Zephaniah 1986: 98)

It is in several anthologies and full details are in the bibliography at the end of the resource pack.

The question is: to correct or not to correct? The pupils can probably find the 'errors' but do they have a right to change the poem?

Group work

Guided reading and writing: teacher-led tasks

Specific to Chapter 1
Focus on:

● Alternative directions: what if the headmaster was the only person who did not think Bill was a girl? What would he say? What would he do?

A Generic
1. Pupils re-read Chapter 1 up to the end of page 12 in turn, privately or with readers taking the parts of the characters and narrator.
2. Teacher-led discussion on the possible courses of action that the head might take.
3. Pupils work in pairs to plan and draft a paragraph describing the head's actions.
4. Teacher comments on and advises pupils on the content of the paragraph. As well as the ideas put forward by pupils the teacher should advise on sentence structure, spelling, punctuation and the use of conjunctions.
5. Pupils complete a paragraph.

(This may provide suitable material for display and/or a plenary session.)

B Supported
1. Pupils either listen to Chapter 1 on audio-tape while reading, or re-read taking the parts with the teacher acting as the narrator.
2. Teacher identifies and asks pupils to identify the paragraphs in the text by noting the first and last words and the way the first word is indented.
3. Teacher-led discussion on the possible courses of action that the head might take.
4. Teacher scribes a draft outline which pupils complete individually or in pairs, or the teacher scribes (or uses ICT resources) an entire paragraph.

(This could be used for display or a plenary).

C Extension
1. Pupils re-read Chapter 1 up to the end of page 12 in turn, privately or with readers taking the parts of the characters and narrator.
2. Teacher-led discussion on the possible courses of action that the head might take.

3. Pupils as individuals plan, draft and write a paragraph describing the head's actions, with teacher advice and support on content and structure.
4. The feasibility of the ideas should be discussed and evaluated as a teacher-led group exercise from one or both of the following perspectives:

- author intention;
- the head as a character in the book.

Guided writing
Focus on:

- Narrative time: how long does it take for events to unfold in the book?
- Reading time: how long does it take to read a page/chapter/the book?

(This task can be used after reading Chapter 1 but is not chapter specific.)

A Generic

1. Pupils read the following poem:

Sleepless Night

I woke up at one
the night had begun.

I woke up at two
the moon in full view.

I woke up at three
a whispering tree.

I woke up at four
saw a shooting star soar.

I woke up at five
when the birds come alive.

I woke up at six
when the tom cats do tricks.

I woke up at seven
saw the moonsun in heaven

I woke up at eight
I don't want to be late . . .
for breakfast!

(John Rice 1991)

2. The teacher-led discussion should lead pupils to the recognition that the poem describes a very long night, but in a few words, and can be read in a short time.
3. This should lead into a teacher-led discussion about the ways in which time unfolds differently in the book. It may take a week to be read to the class but describes the events of one day.
4. Pupils use *Sleepless Night* as a model to write their own poem about a long day.

B Supported
1. As above up to point 3.
2. At point 3, other examples of texts which exemplify the ways in which narrative time can differ from real time should be included.
3. If pupils cannot use *Sleepless Night* as a model, provide a writing frame either on a prepared work-sheet or using ICT. For example:

    At 8 o'clock . . . At 9 o'clock . . .

4. *Sleepless Night* could be typed or scanned into the computer and pupils can edit it.

C Extension
1. As above up to point 3.
2. Pupils should be encouraged to be less dependent on *Sleepless Night* as a model by being encouraged to use other poem forms. The first section of *does w trouble you?*, edited by Gerard Benson (1995) contains examples of lots of different ways to use rhyme including interlacing rhymes and rhymes inside lines. In this way pupils could identify *Sleepless Night* as a poem with rhyming couplets (almost) and then select another rhyme form.

Independent group work

Word/sentence level: time words
This work can be linked to Chapters 1 and 3 and used on a carousel basis.

The issue of time has been a major theme of the work on *Bill's New Frock*. For this reason pupils have been asked to explore within the text, from their own knowledge and with the aid of a dictionary, words and phrases which express the passing of time.

A

Time words

1. You will be working on Chapter —.

2. Find words and phrases that are about time passing slowly, or things happening slowly and write them into the table below.

3. Do the same thing for words and phrases about time passing quickly or things happening quickly.

Time passing slowly or things happening slowly	Time passing quickly or things happening quickly

B

Time words

Read through Chapter —.
Choose some words from the box to put in the chart underneath.
You are looking for words that have something to do with time passing slowly or quickly for Bill.

Some have been done for you.

rushing	*it was a long wait*	ran
hurried	get your skates on	quickly
hurry along	spread like wildfire	charged past
dawdling	couldn't last for ever	ages
hurry back	sitting so still for so long	two minutes later
took his time	heart-stopping rush	a lot faster
couldn't go on	snail-slow progress	race
slowed himself up	not moving fast enough	it didn't last for long
slowly	shot away	slow his pace
sped away	endless	
the clock hands seemed to crawl		

Time passing slowly or things happening slowly	Time passing quickly or things happening quickly
Dawdling	rushing
it was a long wait	

C

Time words

1. You will be working on Chapter —.
2. Find words and phrases that are about time passing slowly, or things happening slowly and write them into the table below.
3. Do the same thing for words and phrases about time passing quickly or things happening quickly.

Time passing slowly or things happening slowly	Time passing quickly or things happening quickly
Dawdling	rushing
it was a long wait	

4. Think of some words or phrases of your own. Use a dictionary to help you.

Time passing slowly or things happening slowly	Time passing quickly or things happening quickly

5. Write a paragraph describing the way Bill feels about his long day.

A

I don't believe it!!!

Throughout the book Bill expresses despair, dismay and disbelief, although there is one bright spot in Chapter 5 when he escapes being blamed for the fight. The tasks enable pupils to explore the range of vocabulary which expresses these feelings and provides a focus for skimming and scanning the text.

Bill could not believe what was happening to him. Read through Chapter — and find words or phrases to put in the boxes below which tell us how he felt. Draw Bill's face in the circles. You can choose:

● things he said out loud;
● things he thought to himself;
● words used by Anne Fine which describe his feelings.

One has been done for you and is in Chapter 2.

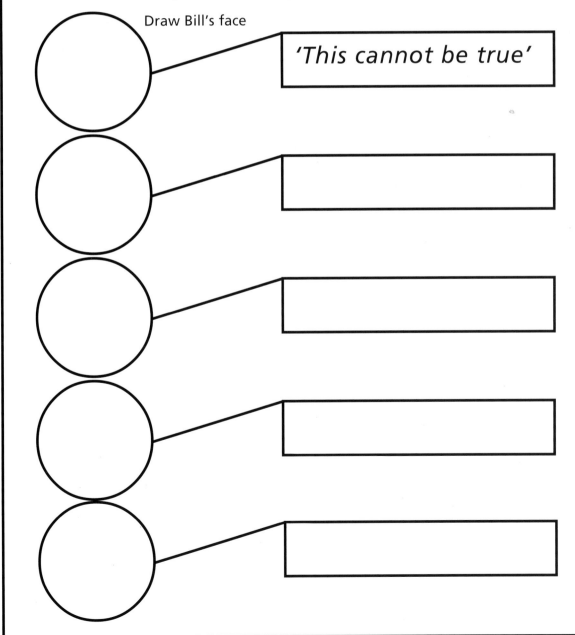

Draw Bill's face

'This cannot be true'

B (based on Chapter 1)

I don't believe it!!!

Read the sentences below.
Put a ✔ next to things you think Bill did say or think.
Put a ✘ next to things you think Bill didn't say or think.

Did Bill say or think it?	✔ or ✘
This cannot be true!	
Great, I'm a girl.	
I wish this pink dress was blue.	
He felt so foolish . . .	
Oh, this was awful!	
I'm not the only one in a dress.	
Oh, no! Oh, no!	
It's great reading Rapunzel.	

C

I don't believe it!!!

Write a paragraph describing how Bill feels. Plan your work in the box below.

Notes and ideas

Chapter 2

The Wumpy Choo

Characters	Settings	Events	Comments
Bill Simpson	Playground	Couldn't join boys playing football	
Boys	Playground		
Girls	Playground	Bill observes girls' behaviour in the playground	
Leila, Kirsty, Astrid, Flora, Linda, Talilah		They discuss kicking the ball through an open window and decide they could	It's a matter of opportunity
	Playground	Bill isn't given access to the football game in the way he expected	
Rohan & Martin	Playground	Demand ball back and tell Bill to go to his own bit – however they dare not fight for the ball	
Bill	Playground	Bill wins 1p chew by default and is humiliated	

Whole-class shared text work

Focus areas for discussion:

- Playing areas in the playground.
- Games played by boys and girls and playground issues.
- Narrative time and reading time.

Text level: alternative endings

The ending of Chapter 2 is quite interesting. It is very downbeat as Bill's playtime gets worse and worse. In some ways the playtime is a microcosm of the whole day. He cannot do what he usually does; he cannot quite get to grips with what is going on around him; and his misunderstanding of what a 'wumpy choo' is leads to his final humiliation.

The short extract and the question can promote a lot of discussion about Bill as a character and Anne Fine as an author. If you asked pupils to predict the ending of the chapter how many would opt for him triumphantly kicking the ball through the window? In narrative terms, it would not be an unreasonable prediction. Also, notice how Bill displays a stereotypical characteristic of a boy: he is not going to cry in front of everybody. The questions that accompany this extract are:

1. Why did this chapter end in the way it did?
2. Should Anne Fine let Bill have 'show them'?

In silence, Bill Simpson turned and walked away. If all the girls had not been standing around the edges of the playground watching him, he would have cried. (p. 33)

Text level: issues of understanding

Using a related text:
In Peter Dixon's book *Grow Your Own Poems* (1988) there is a poem called 'Fatty Melville'. The first few lines are:

Fatty Melville

pop out eyes

Fatty Melville

he's got flies

(Dixon 1988: 23)

Dixon writes that it's a sad poem, that Fatty Melville went to his school, and that he hopes children are kinder now.

These are good discussion points to link with this chapter and Chapter 6, 'Letting Paul Win'.

Word/sentence/text level: the semantic field* of menacing words

Use from page 29, the final paragraph: 'The footballers gathered', to page 32, the end of paragraph 3: 'with fiddly shell buttons'. The words or phrases to focus on are:

menacing   narrowed eyes   scowling   glowering

1. Either ask pupils to identify 'menacing' words and phrases from the text which can be underlined by the teacher; or
2. Provide the text already highlighted and ask pupils what links the words together.

Sentence level: sentence structure and conditional forms

1. Exploring alternative endings to Chapter 2 at text level can be linked to the sentence level work of exploring conditional forms, e.g. if/would and if/then.
2. Using the framework below on OHT or whiteboard, the teacher can write in suggestions from the class:

If all the girls had not been watching he would have cried.
If he had kicked the ball through the window he would have ———.
If he had played girls' games ———.
If he had known what a wumpy choo was ———.

Word level: vocabulary related to conditional forms

Conditional forms are useful for exploring ways in which characters and/or the course of events can be sure and definite or indecisive. Use the table below as a **substitution table** to discuss the effect the alternative forms could have on the

---

* A semantic field is a group of words or phrases identified in a text which are linked together by meaning. The words do not have to belong to the same word class and they are a form of *lexical cohesion*. The direct repetition of the words 'girls were' is also a form of lexical cohesion. These are often referred to as *cohesive ties*.

text. This also links with exploring and expressing alternative endings and directions. I have taken events from Chapters 1 and 2, but other chapters provide plenty of opportunities for this aspect of sentence construction.

Ask pupils to say their sentences out loud so that they can listen to and hear the different effects. Some of the nuances in meaning are very subtle and it needs different expression and intonation to really bring out these differences. You could try a short role play or some dialogue work at this point, with one pupil starting off with a sentence constructed from the chart.

If Bill had taken the dress off . . .	he might have . . . he would have . . .	had a very different day.
If Bill had said something disagreeable to the old lady . . .	she might have been . . . she would have been . . . she could have been . . .	very upset. very cross. surprised.
If the headmaster had chosen some girls . . .	Astrid might have been . . . Astrid would have been . . .	very pleased. chosen.
If Bill wasn't wearing a dress . . .	he wouldn't have . . . he couldn't have . . .	joined the girls in the playground.
If Bill had given the ball back . . .	he would never have . . . he could never have . . . he might never have . . .	known what a wumpy choo was.

Example from the text

If you looked back through the last pages of the his work, you'd see he'd done a really good job, for him. (p. 16)

In addition there is an elided form *you'd* which can be used to ask the questions:

1. What is the full form?
2. What if it were *you could* or *you should*? How would this affect the meaning of the text?

Word level: spelling

Using the work on menacing words is useful for exploring the different ways in which *ow* can be pronounced. Listed below are several directions this type of word work could take:

> narrowed eyes　　scowling　　glowering

1. Focus on *ow*.
2. Different pronunciation of *ow*.
3. Extend the list of *ow* words
4. Make several *ow* cards and either provide further cards to make complete words, e.g. *b, bl, br, c, cr, ed, ing* and so on. Distribute them to pupils and ask them to form themselves into words, or distribute blank cards on which pupils can write their own ideas and then see if they work.
5. Use other letter combinations in the same range. e.g. *ou*, cloud, round etc.
6. Extend the range of *ou* words, e.g. bought, wound etc.
7. As an extension of 5, you could look at the wide range of *ough* words, e.g. bought, brought, thought, fought etc.

Group work

Guided reading and writing: teacher-led tasks

Specific to Chapter 2: alternative endings

A Generic
1. Pupils re-read Chapter 2, pages 32 and 33, privately or as a guided reading exercise.
2. The teacher-led discussion, drawing on the whole-class work, should take pupils through Bill's puzzlement and anger to the rather anticlimactic ending.
3. Pupils plan, draft and write with teacher guidance, a paragraph with an upbeat ending to the chapter.

B Supported
1. As generic up to point 3.
2. Teacher should act as a scribe or use ICT resources to produce an agreed alternative upbeat ending.

C Extension
1. As generic up to and including point 3.
2. Pupils should explore the ending from the perspectives of characterisation and author intention. Returning to the theme of the whole class work, in many books Bill would have 'shown them' by kicking the ball through the open window, but Anne Fine did not let him. Why did Bill not know what a wumpy choo was? He seemed to be the only person who heard '1p chew' as 'wumpy choo'. Even when he repeated the words to Martin, Martin heard it as '1p chew'. Is this a weak point in the story? What about the issue of Martin not wanting to fight Bill for the ball? There are a lot of questions worth exploring with a group which would draw on pupils' own experiences and could eventually lead on to the ending possibly being 'more real' than a happy ending.

Note: These are examples of endings produced by two year 6 pupils:

1. Bill felt very mad but he just said this is the best thing I ever had.
2. This made Bill mad. He storms back into the pitch, picks the football up and boots it into Martin's face, who then puts out his fists and punches Bill in the face. Then Bill kicked back and Martin went flying into the wall. All the girls started shouting, 'Girls are best! Girls are best!'

Independent group tasks

Sentence level/text level: toys for boys and toys for girls
This work can be linked to Chapter 2 and used on a carousel basis.

Toys often clearly target boys or girls. This activity enables pupils to consider a gender issue which is directly relevant to them and can be exploited as a means of accessing other gender issues raised in the book. It links quite well with Chapter 2 and the issue of who owns the space in the playground. The task is designed at two levels only, as most pupils should be able to undertake the sorting and discussion task. The chart for level C could be used in a plenary session to show examples of well-constructed sentences or to focus on common errors.

Independent group task

Resources:

- a large selection of pictures of toys pasted on to card

- a large card marked into large circles and labelled:

  Toys for boys

  Toys for girls

- where the circles overlap mark it as:

  Toys for boys or girls.

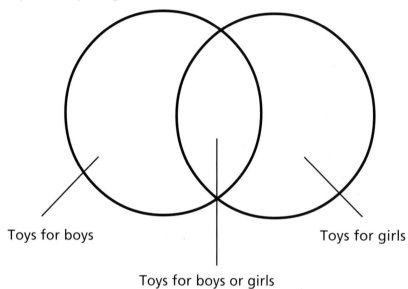

Toys for boys   Toys for girls

Toys for boys or girls

A/B

Toys for boys and toys for girls

- Put all the toy picture cards face down in the middle of the table or desk.

- Take it in turns to pick one up.

- Put the card in the 'Toys for boys' or 'Toys for girls' or 'Toys for boys and girls' space on the big card BUT you must say why you are putting the card on the space you choose.

- When you have finished, decide which toys the characters in the story would like most.

- Write them in the name spaces below.

- If you have not heard of any of the characters yet, leave them out.

Kirsty	Mean Malcolm	Talilah

Philip	Astrid

C

Toys for boys and toys for girls

Finish the chart:

A lego set is	a good toy for a boy or girl because	all children like making their own toys
Pencil crayons are	a good toy for a boy or girl because	most children like drawing and colouring
	a good toy for a boy or girl because	
	a good toy for a boy or girl because	
	a good toy for a boy or girl because	
	a good toy for a boy or girl because	

Do you think there should be toys just for boys and just for girls? You must give a reason for your answer. Write a short paragraph.

_____

_____

_____

_____

_____

Chapter 3

Pink, Pink, Nothing but Pink

Characters	Settings	Events	Comments
Mrs Collins	Classroom	Painting lesson	
Leila			
Kirsty		Expresses her disgust at the excess of pink paint	
Bill	Classroom	Resists Mrs Collins's attempts to take him to the chair. Resistance leads to accident with paint	Mrs Collins is surprised that Bill resists
Bill	Classroom	Resigns himself	Compares himself with Rapunzel

Whole-class shared text work

Focus areas for discussion

Prepare the text from page 38, last paragraph: 'Bill tried to pull back', to page 39, end of paragraph 2: 'beside his left foot', for display to the whole class.

● Gender issues: Mrs Collins' surprise as Bill resists being taken to the chair; why was she surprised? This may start a discussion on the different expectations teachers have of boys' and girls' behaviour.
● Would Mrs Collins have been less surprised if a boy had pulled away from her?
● Bill's shifting thoughts from resistance to compliance.

Text level: cause and effect/summarising/new paragraphs

1. Identify the start and finish of each paragraph. Is it based on 'new paragraph, new idea'? (You may want to discuss the indent/do not indent debate.)
2. Ask for suggestions to write on the whiteboard on how to summarise the sequence of events.

Text level/sentence/word level; following the shifting thoughts of a character

Prepare page 40, paragraph 4: 'Bill Simpson . . . hoping for rescue'.

1. Is this the point where Bill began to come to terms with his day? Has he lost all fight, all resistance?
2. What words and phrases in the text provide evidence for this?
3. What metaphor is used to describe the progress of the day?
4. Note the reference to Chapter 1: Rapunzel.

Whole-class work

Sentence level: conditional forms

1. Develop knowledge of terminology of conditional forms by putting the incomplete sentences below on display for pupils to complete.
2. Provide pupils with small whiteboards or clipboard so that they can work in pairs to complete the sentences.

3. Complete the sentences using suggestions from the pupils.

   If Bill hadn't tried to pull back . . .
   If Mrs Collins hadn't suddenly let go of Bill's hand . . .
   If Nicky hadn't just prised the top off his paint tub . . .

Word/sentence level: vocabulary extension

Semantic fields: words and phrases relating to compliance and lack of resistance. The selection below come from page 40: 'Bill Simpson could have tried . . . hoping for rescue':

   didn't bother
   no point
   give up
   trapped
   sit quietly

1. Put the paragraph on to the whiteboard, OHT etc. with the phrases above omitted. Pupils can have cards with phrases written on and hold them up at the appropriate point during the reading of the paragraph.
2. Discuss what links the words together; that is, Bill's mood, which is close to despair.
3. Scribe some sentences on to the whiteboard which include and illustrate these words.

Group work

Guided reading and writing: teacher-led tasks

Sentence level: summarising, revising sentence structure

A Generic

1. Re-read or listen to chapter up to the end of page 37.
2. Identify simple, compound and complex sentences.
3. Identify main and subordinate clauses.
4. Identify conjunctions; mainly *and*, *but* and *so*.
5. Identify the most important parts of this extract to summarise into no more than two paragraphs.

Simple sentences	Compound sentences	Complex sentences
There *must* be crayons.	The infants came and borrowed ours last week, and haven't brought them back yet.	Everyone gazed around the room, looking for something that was all pink so they could paint it.
Every class has crayons.	So Leila dragged the heavy cardboard box full of paint tubs out of the cupboard, and everyone crowded round to choose their colours.	And taking Bill Simpson firmly by the hand, she tried to lead him over towards a chair in the middle of the room, where everyone would be able to see him clearly while they were painting him.

This table provides some examples, if required.

Main clause	Subordinate clause
Everyone gazed around the room	
she tried to lead him over towards a chair in the middle of the room,	where everyone would be able to see him clearly
	while they were painting him.

(p. 35)

B Supported
1. Re-read or listen to chapter up to the end of page 37.
2. Teacher support to identify simple, compound and complex sentences.
3. Teacher support to identify conjunctions; mainly *and*, *but* and *so*.
4. Identify the most important parts of this extract to summarise into no more than two paragraphs, teacher acting as scribe if necessary.

C Extension
1. Re-read up to the end of page 37.
2. Identify simple, compound and complex sentences.
3. Identify main and subordinate clauses.
4. Find the conjunctions *and*, *but*, *so*.
5. Discuss their function in enabling the text to flow.
6. Present pupils with a chart of different categories of conjunction and their function.
7. Identify the most important parts of this extract to summarise into no more than two paragraphs.
8. Refer back to conjunctions; how can different effects be achieved?

The chart overleaf has been adapted from *Working with Texts* by Ronald Carter *et al.* (1997) and further information has been added underneath about conjunctions. The main adaptation to the chart has been to the wording under the heading *Meaning*, to try and make it more accessible to key stage 2 pupils. However, there are some quite complex concepts to grasp. The extended version of the task on sentence structure (see above) looks at the ways in which conjunctions have an important function, not just in sentence structure but also meaning. If pupils can get to grips with the ways in which conjunctions work it can help to add to the flow, style and clarity of their writing. If you do decide to use this task you might like to omit the first column, *Type of conjunction*, and use it for your information only. Many of the examples can be found in information texts, particularly non-chronological, non-narrative texts when conjunctions are essential to make the text cohesive. The tasks suggested above should be seen as part of a long-term strategy and returned to when using non-fiction texts for literacy hours. There is an alternative version of this chart linked to an independent group task which you may prefer to use.

Type of conjunction	Meaning	Examples
additives/ alternatives	Use these conjunctions if you want to give some more information	and/or/furthermore/in addition/ likewise/in other words
adversative	Use these conjunctions if you want to add some different, perhaps opposite information	but/yet /though/however/on the contrary
causal	Use these conjunctions if you want to explain why something happened or write about what happens next	so/then/for/this reason consequently/it follows that/ as a result
temporal	Use these conjunctions if you want to show how time is passing in your writing	one day/then/finally/up to now/ the next day/while
continuatives	Use these conjunctions if you are writing a new sentence but want to keep writing about the same idea	well/now/of course/anyway surely/after all

(adapted from Carter, R. *et al*:217)

Subordinating conjunctions:
> after, although, as, because, before, but, if, how, however, like, once, since, than, that, till, unless, until, when, whenever, wherever, whereas, whereby, whereupon, while, in that, so that, in order that, except that, as far as, as soon as, rather than, as if, as though, in case.

Co-ordinating conjunctions:
> and, or, but, neither.

(Leech *et al.* 1982: 52)

Independent group tasks
(see also those listed under Chapters 1 and 2)

Word/sentence level: conjunctions
For use with Chapter 3 but can also be adapted to use on a carousel basis.

The task looks at how conjunctions have been used in one extract of text and could easily be transferred to other extracts with a greater range of conjunctions. As well as looking at the grammatical function of conjunctions, pupils should be encouraged to consider how they link ideas together and aid the flow of the text. I alluded earlier to a possible conflict in the way Anne Fine uses 'and' and the need to enable pupils to use conjunctions other than 'and'. You can use the tasks below to talk about this particular problem.

Note: This task is linked to the guided writing task for Chapter 3 and pupils may find the concepts and terminology in the chart above quite difficult. I have provided the complete version of this chart in the guided writing section for information, but suggested a simplified version below for use with pupils both for this task and the guided writing task.

A

Generic

Lots of ands and buts!

Conjunctions help to join clauses and sentences together, and they also join a writer's ideas together. The sentences below come from page 37 "And Kirsty looked at Bill" to page 38 ". . . a really fine portrait of him."

Conjunctions	Meaning
and or furthermore in addition likewise in other words	Use these conjunctions if you want to give some more information.
but yet though however on the contrary	Use these conjunctions if you want to add some different, perhaps opposite information.
so then for this reason consequently it follows that as a result	Use these conjunctions if you want to explain why something happened or write about what happens next.
one day then finally up to now the next day while	Use these conjunctions if you want to show how time is passing in your writing.
well now of course anyway surely after all	Use these conjunctions if you are writing a new sentence but want to keep writing about the same idea.

(Adapted from Carter, R. *et al*: 217)

1. Look at the conjunctions chart and find *and/now/but* in the Conjunctions column.

   ● Look at the other conjunctions. Could you use any of them instead of *and* or *now* or *but*? Try them out to see if they look and sound right.
   ● What about '*However* he was getting pinker by the minute'? Does it sound and look right?

2. Work in pairs and choose another conjunction to swap with the conjunction in italics in the table overleaf.

Look at the conjunction in italics	Choose a new conjunction and try it out
And Kirsty looked at Bill.	though but so finally
Now everyone turned to look at Bill.	well anyway for this reason likewise
Now even Mrs. Collins was looking at Bill.	after all surely finally then
But he was getting pinker by the minute.	of course in addition yet in other words

3. Read the piece from the story aloud putting in the conjunction you have chosen. Does it still make sense?

- If not, can you put in a conjunction of your own so that it *will* make sense. Have you got to use Anne Fine's choice?
- Can you find any other conjunctions in the piece?

B

LOTS OF ANDS AND BUTS!

Word/sentence level: conjunctions

Extract from Chapter 3: Pink, Pink, Nothing but Pink
Use from page 37: 'And Kirsty looked at Bill', to page 38: ' "Perfect," said Mrs Collins.'

Support task: grammatical cloze procedure
Cloze procedure passages are often prepared by deleting every ninth word; this usually gives pupils the opportunity of inserting words from many different word classes. With grammatical cloze you select one, possibly two word classes to delete. The missing words should *not* be listed underneath the text. If pupils are having real difficulty provide a choice of words on small cards (small enough to fit into the spaces on the text).
   The extract from Chapter 3 has *and, now* and *but* as the main conjunctions:

1. Prepare the passage by deleting the conjunctions you would like the pupils to focus on.
2. Speaking and listening can be incorporated into this task by allowing pupils in the group to work in pairs to agree on the missing words.
3. Pupils can compare their text with the original on completing it.

Note: If pupils produce a version which is different from the original, they can consider which version they prefer. They should try reading both out loud before making a decision.

C

Your own writing

Advice and instructions to pupils could take the following form:
- Write a letter from Bill to a friend describing what happened when the other pupils painted him.
- Think about paragraphs and conjunctions.
- In real life, you do not often plan and draft letters, but you need to for this work. You might change your mind about when your paragraphs start and finish, how to write your sentences and which conjunctions to use.
- Don't forget to write your **address**, **Dear —**, and to think of the best way of ending the letter. For example, would you write **Yours sincerely**?

Chapter 4

No Pockets

Characters	Settings	Events	Comments
Mrs Collins	Classroom	Gives Bill a job and an excuse to leave the classroom	
Bill	Corridor	Dilemma of the boys' or girls' toilets	
Headmaster	Corridor	Praises his demeanour and gives him another job	
School nurse	Corridor	Gives him another job but assumes he does not mind	
Bill	Corridor	Discovers he has no pockets	Detail and description of dress – care but no pockets (p. 49)
Caretaker	Corridor	Adds tennis balls to the pile	
Mrs Bandaraina	Corridor/office	Her comment about care and the sweet little pink dress is the last straw. He drops everything	

Whole-class shared text work

Focus areas for discussion

- Predicting what would happen next in the sequence of events.
- The lack of pockets and clothing in general.
- Continue with narrative time and reading time.

Whole class work

Word level: vocabulary extension – proverbs

Proverbs and sayings are often seen as a rather trite and clichéd response to events and situations. The meanings of proverbs are often puzzling to pupils and certainly the year 6 class who tried these tasks found them difficult to interpret. Proverbs can be useful for looking at figurative language. For example, *the last straw breaks the camel's back* paints a vivid mental picture of a camel with its knees buckling and its hump caving in as one last piece of straw is loaded on. Proverbs cross time and boundaries. We may not use camels for transport in Britain, and they may be used less as transport in deserts, but it is these facts which make proverbs part of learning about figurative language.

Proverbs can summarise quite complex situations in a few words and *Bill's New Frock* provides some paragraphs which can be effectively summarised in this way. (An extensive list of proverbs, sayings and adages can be found on the internet at http://www.coloacad.org/libraries/adages.html.)

1. Present the class with a selection of proverbs and sayings on OHT, whiteboard etc.

> Actions speak louder than words
> Little things please little minds
> Least said soonest mended
> The last straw breaks the camel's back
> All's well that ends well
> An apple a day keeps the doctor away
> Nothing ventured nothing gained
> You cannot have your cake and eat it
> A stitch in time saves nine
> Every cloud has a silver lining
> It's a long lane that has no turning
> Honesty is the best policy
> Listeners hear no good of themselves
> One good turn deserves another
> More haste less speed
> Prevention is better than cure
> A watched pot never boils

2. Discuss the meanings of the proverbs and ask for additions to the list.
3. Identify any that are relevant to the story.
4. Present a selection of paragraphs from the story and ask pupils to suggest a summarising proverb. One way to do this would be to have the proverbs printed on to card so that pupils could fetch their choice.
5. Take the discussion on to what the proverb means and why it does summarise the paragraph.

I have listed below a few sample paragraphs and suggested proverbs:

> Outside, in the deserted corridor, one thought and one thought only was in Bill Simpson's mind: lavatories! Silently he crept along. Should he turn left, into the BOYS, and risk hoots and catcalls of astonishment if anyone caught him there in his pretty pink frock? Or should he turn right, into the GIRLS, where for a boy even to be found hanging around the doorway was to risk terrible trouble? (p. 45)
> **Nothing ventured nothing gained.**

> Then he tried to pull himself together. This couldn't last forever. This couldn't go on. No boy could turn into a girl and stay that way without anyone – even his mother and teacher and schoolfriends – noticing any real difference. It must be a bad dream. It *felt* like a nightmare . . . (p. 50)
> **It's a long lane that has no turning.**

> 'My!' Mrs Bandaraina said, watching his snail-slow progress. 'Aren't you the careful one, taking care not to spill coloured ink on your sweet little frock!' (p. 52)
> **The last straw breaks the camel's back.**

Group work

Guided reading and writing: teacher-led tasks

Text level: sequencing paragraphs

A/C Generic/extension
1. Pupils should have access to Chapter 4 for reference.
2. Provide the whole group or sub-groups with paragraphs from the chapter cut out and placed on to card which describe the sequence of events from when Bill emerges from the toilet and is given his first job until the disaster in Mrs Bandaraina's office.
3. With teacher support pupils should work co-operatively to sequence the paragraphs correctly.
4. A teacher-led discussion should lead to suggestions based on pupil experience for other jobs that Bill might have been asked to do.
5. With teacher support pupils can write a list of jobs, incorporating their own ideas into the list of jobs Bill had to do.

B Supported
1. The teacher should read or use the audio-tape version to support the sequencing of the paragraphs.
2. The teacher should scribe suggestions for other jobs that Bill might have to do.
3. The teacher should scribe the final extended list.

Text level: switching genre
(Can be used with other chapters)
This task has always worked well. Pupils start with a short extract of text providing all the language they need so you, the teacher, can then focus all their attention on the shape of the poem, the way the language should be manipulated and, as suggested in the extension activity, to guide pupils to one of the many poem forms suggested in the literacy strategy. Further helpful resources would be a selection of poetry books which provide a range of examples of poems. One such book is *does w trouble you?*, edited by Gerard Benson (1955). The poems can be read in plenary sessions.

A Generic
1. Pupils select a small piece of text from the chapter.
2. With teacher-led help and advice they re-work the text through the planning, drafting and editing process into a group poem.

B Supported
1. Pupils use pre-selected pieces of text.
2. With teacher-led help and advice they re-work the text through the planning, drafting and editing process into a group poem.
3. If necessary, a model such as the one below can be provided using page 49, paragraph 2: 'No. Not one pocket . . . puffy little sleeves'.

> *No Pockets*
> Yards and yards of material
> But no pockets.
> Pleats, frills and bows
> But no pockets.
> Lots of lace around the hem,
> Lots of lace around the neck,
> But no pockets!!
> A nice zip and pretty sleeves
> BUT NO POCKETS!!!!!!!

C Extension
1. Pupils complete the task as for the generic version **but**, with teacher support and guidance, they must select an identifiable poem form. For example, go back to the various rhyme forms when pupils were using 'Sleepless Night' in the Chapter 1 work.
2. Teach any rules or conventions of the chosen poem form as part of the task. (The National Literacy Strategy glossary provides guidance but you will probably need a selection of poetry books.)
3. 'Sleepless Night' ends by breaking away from the rhyming couplet format. If pupils are using a form which does have a regular and repetitive structure, they could think about ending the poem by breaking away from that structure.

The poem below was written by a Year 6 pupil based on text on page 47 when the head teacher gave Bill the ink bottles:

>The Errand
>
>The head-teacher gave me an errand.
>I didn't want to go,
>'Don't dawdle, don't look at paintings.'
>I don't want to go.
>Don't drop the yellow, pink, blue
>Ink bottles please.
>I don't want to do it.

Independent group tasks

Word/sentence/text level: proverbs and sayings
This task has been linked to Chapter 4. Add further paragraphs as indicated below to continue using the task during the week.

This task is linked to the whole-class teaching on proverbs and gives the pupils an opportunity to summarise with a proverb. In the A task you could try giving pupils more proverbs than meanings to promote discussion. They will need the list of proverbs for the B task which follows.

A

What do proverbs mean?

Working in pairs, write the number of the proverb in the box next to the right meaning:

Proverb meaning	Number
Think about something before you do it.	
Silly people do dangerous things.	
If you do a job now it will be done much quicker than if you leave it.	
Even if things go wrong, it's OK if it turns out all right in the end.	
The things that you do are more important than the things that you say.	
If you eat healthy food you will not be ill.	
Looking after yourself is better than having to take medicine.	
The more you hurry and rush, the longer it takes to do things.	
Quiet people think about things a lot.	
Even when things are really bad, you can still find something to be happy about.	
It is best to always tell the truth.	
Enjoy yourself while you can.	
If you listen to somebody talking about you, you will not hear anything good.	
Important and great things can start from very small beginnings.	
Somebody who never stays in one place for very long never gets rich.	
If you do not think carefully before you get married, you will have a long time to think about the mistake you have made.	
Sometimes it is better to have what you have got rather than nothing at all	

B

Proverbs and sayings

Read through these proverbs with a partner.

Put a ✔ next to any of the proverbs which might have something to do with the story.

You might not understand all of them. If you don't understand the proverb put a ✗ next to it.

1. Actions speak louder than words.

2. All's well that ends well.

3. An apple a day keeps the doctor away.

4. A stitch in time saves nine.

5. A bird in the hand is worth two in the bush.

6. A rolling stone gathers no moss.

7. Every cloud has a silver lining.

8. Fools rush in where angels fear to tread.

9. Great oaks from little acorns grow.

10. Honesty is the best policy.

11. Listeners hear no good of themselves.

12. Look before you leap.

13. Great minds think alike.

14. One good turn deserves another.

15. Marry in haste and repent at leisure.

16. Make hay while the sun shines.

17. More haste less speed.

18. Necessity is the mother of invention.

19. Prevention is better than cure.

20. Still waters run deep.

C

Proverbs and *Bill's New Frock*

Summarise these paragraphs from *Bill's New Frock* with a proverb.
You can choose one from the list or use one that you know.

Chapter 3: Pink, Pink, Nothing but Pink (page 38):

Bill tried to pull back. Mrs Collins turned in astonishment at his unwillingness, and let go of his hand quite suddenly. Bill staggered back – straight into Nicky who had just prised the top off his paint tub.

| *Proverb* |
| |
| |
| |

Chapter 4: No Pockets (page 47):
Bill Simpson started looking sharp. Lifting his chin, he walked a lot faster. He was almost safely past the headmaster when he was stopped.

| *Proverb* |
| |
| |
| |

Page 50:
This couldn't go on. No boy could turn into a girl and stay that way without anyone – even his mother and teacher and schoolfriends – noticing any real difference. It must be a bad dream. It felt like a nightmare . . .

| *Proverb* |
| |
| |
| |

Chapter 5: The Big Fight (pages 58–9):
Bill glanced down at the comic in his hands. He didn't care for the look of it at all. He didn't want to read it. What use was a *Bunty*? He wanted a *Beano* or a *Dandy* or a *Thunder*, and that was that.

| *Proverb* |
| |
| |
| |

Chapter 6: Letting Paul Win (page 86):
'It doesn't matter,' Kirsty said. 'In fact it was probably all for the best. If he'd come first, Paul might have guessed.'

| *Proverb* |
| |
| |
| |

Chapter 5

The Big Fight

Characters	Settings	Events	Comments
Mrs Collins		Wet lunch hour put her in a bad mood	Poem forms on moods?
Bill	Classroom in wet lunchtime	He's given a *Bunty* comic	
Melissa & Flora		Reading *Dandy* or *Beano* and won't swap	
Rohan & Martin		Reading *Valiant* and *Victor* and won't swap	
Bill Simpson		Surprised to find himself enjoying *Bunty*. Reluctantly swaps it for a *Dandy*	Story outlines (p. 62) as possible models for writing?
Rohan		Wants Bill to swap his *Dandy* for a *June*. Assumes Bill will prefer *June*.	
Bill & Rohan		Fight over comics	
Mrs Simpson		Breaks up fight and assumes Bill is in the right	It all hinges on the footprint on the dress (p. 68)
Bill and Rohan		Write lines	Bill is said to look upset, while Rohan is said to look angry – possible word level work

Whole-class shared text work

Focus areas for discussion:

- Bill's discovery that being seen as a girl has its advantages.
- Real life wet dinner times.
- Continue pointing out narrative time and reading time.

Whole-class work: shared reading and writing

Sentence level: return to conditional forms

The fight in Chapter 5 had to happen. Bill's frustration and bewilderment had to explode eventually. His bewilderment increased as he actually found himself enjoying a comic that was meant for girls. Of course, the fight could have been avoided in all sorts of ways, and it is because of this that this is an ideal chapter to explore conditional sentences in more depth.

Prepare from page 61, final paragraph: 'Bill blamed Mrs Collins', to page 62, end of second paragraph: 'all the same' and add the sentences underneath as follows:

If Mrs Collins had not given Bill a *Bunty* then . . .
If Bill had shared the *Valiant* with Rohan then . . .

1. Use the paragraph for reading with the class.
2. Ask pupils to finish the sentences. Pupils can work in pairs, writing their sentences on a small whiteboard or clipboard.
3. Revise the terminology relating to conditional forms and discuss their purpose and function in a text.

In addition prepare page 63 from 'Here. You take this', to page 64: 'tried to snatch it'. Highlight '**And Bill shook his *Dandy* in Rohan's face. That was his first big mistake. His second big mistake was not moving fast enough when Rohan reached out and tried to snatch it**' (p. 64).

1. Use the paragraph for reading with the class. Pupils can read this with appropriate expression and intonation, or it can be acted out.
2. Change the sentences in bold into conditional forms. For example:

   If Bill hadn't shaken his *Dandy* in Rohan's face the fight wouldn't have started.
   If Bill had moved faster Rohan couldn't have snatched it.

Word level
Prepare the final paragraph on page 62: 'Then as the blows', to page 67: 'Never' and add:

   And every now and again, someone would tiptoe past and whisper in Rohan's ear:
     'You look so angry.'
   But in Bill's they whispered:
     'You look so upset.' *(*p. 69)

1. Ask pupils to read the extracts out loud using appropriate intonation and expression.
2. Discuss the significance of the author's choice of words *angry* and *upset*. Boys get angry and girls get upset, or do they?
3. Pupils can list other words or phrases under *angry* and *upset* on a small whiteboard or clipboard and talk about their choices to the remainder of the class.

Group work

Guided reading and writing: teacher-led tasks

Sentence/text level: summarising
So far, the summarising tasks and the identification of paragraphs have been based on the content of *Bill's New Frock*, and as pupils have worked their way through the book they will have become more and more familiar with the themes and issues linked to expectations about behaviour, likes and dislikes, and achievements of boys and girls.

Below is an adaptation of a story in *The Times Educational Supplement*. Angela Phillips asked pupils what they thought about the idea that girls do better than boys at school. It links well with the book, provides a different style of text and opportunities for pupils to transfer themes and issues they have addressed through fiction to non-fiction.

In previous tasks, pupils have been asked to summarise short paragraphs by using proverbs. This task is another approach to summarising. The questions at the top of the chart help pupils to find the main points. There may be other key issues you would like pupils to write about; in this case, simply change the questions and/or add one or two new columns with new questions. The fact that the pupils' notes

are in a table makes it difficult to copy inappropriate chunks from the original text.
   For more information on this approach read Bobbie Neate's *Finding Out about Finding Out* (1992).

A Generic
1. Read the abridged version of 'It's Just So Unfair' by Angela Phillips as a group reading exercise:

> I surveyed 134 London school children to find out what they thought about the idea that girls do better at school than boys. Almost 30% of the girls believed that girls were more intelligent than boys, and surprisingly, nearly 20% of the boys agreed with them.
>
> Many boys believed that teachers favoured girls, but the girls did not agree. However, some girls thought that teachers liked to talk to pupils who worked and behaved, and that was mainly girls.
>
> A lot of boys said it was very difficult to work hard because your friends laughed at you and you did not 'look cool'. They said you could only work hard if you made it look easy.
>
> Some of the boys said they needed their friends, but at the same time it was really hard to work together and help each other in the same way girls do. Even though they needed their friends, they could not admit it and had to pretend they were tough and did not need anybody.
>
> Some boys knew they were showing off in front of their friends and misbehaving in the classroom. They also said they really did want to work harder but they were afraid all their friends would laugh at them.
>
> The school in the survey formed two discussion groups, one for the boys and one for the girls. In the girl's discussion group many of the girls thought that boys would do just as well at school if they helped each other in the same way that girls did. In the boy's group it was very difficult to get the boys to think about themselves. They blamed the girls and then the teachers for not doing well at school, but would not think about their own behaviour. In the end the boys did decide they must help each other more, and more importantly they decided that older boys should work with younger boys to stop them getting into bad habits in the classroom. (Adapted from *The Times Educational Supplement,* 13 November 1998)

2. Discuss the main points of the article with pupils.
3. Provide the chart below for pupils to tabulate the main points:

What do the boys think about the girls' behaviour?	What do the girls think about the boys' behaviour?	What must the boys do to improve their work at school?

4. Reformulate the points to form a summary of the article.

B Supported
1. Read *It's Just So Unfair* as a group reading exercise.
2. Discuss the main points of the article with the pupils.
3. Help pupils to select the main points to go into the chart.
4. Help pupils to produce a summarising paragraph.

C Extended

1. Read the abridged or original article as a group reading exercise.
2. Pupils work in pairs to underline main points in the text and explain their choices to the teacher.
3. Discuss the validity of the points made by the boys and girls in the text.
4. Discuss the ways in which the issues in this text relate to *Bill's New Frock*.
5. Pupils complete the chart and reformulate the points to produce a summarising paragraph.

Independent group work
See tasks listed under Chapters 1–5.

Chapter 6

Letting Paul Win

Characters	Settings	Events	Comments
Mrs Collins	Grass outside	Lots of different races with lots of categories	
Bill, Astrid, Kirsty, Talilah		Arrange to let Paul win	
Bill		Somehow can't let Paul win	
Paul		Delighted at coming second	
Girls		Initially angry with Bill, but decide Paul might have suspected something, so it was OK in the end	Bill has identity crisis

Whole-class shared text work

Focus areas for discussion

- During the reading, predicting the implications of Bill's lack of involvement in the girls' plan.
- Predicting whether or not Bill would let Paul win.
- Discuss the possible reasons why Bill could not let him win.

Text level: the story so far

This is a good point at which to reprise the story so far. The happy ending is on its way; the crisis point of the fight is over; Bill discovered an advantage to being a girl in Chapter 5 and his 'inability to behave like a girl' does not have disastrous consequences. Things are starting to become resolved.

1. Use the whiteboard or other medium to scribe the main events of the story so far.
2. Some or all of the events can be discussed in the context of expectations of boys' and girls' behaviour.
3. List the dirt and damage done to the pink dress. The fingerprints and so on can be written on to card and pupils can stand in the order in which the marks got on to the dress.
4. Discuss the possible ending of the story.

Whole-class work

Word/sentence level: consolidation of conjunctions

Prepare an extract from page 79: 'Up at the front . . . Kirsty wink'.
  These paragraphs communicate the speed of events as the girls take themselves out of the race. Going back to the chart adapted from Carter *et al.* (1997) on conjunctions, these paragraphs show conjunctions at work:

- *Now* and *then* are temporal conjunctions and illustrate nicely the way the girls change places.
- *But*, as an adversative conjunction, indicates quite a change in events, which

comes about as the girls deliberately tangle themselves up.

- *As* is not listed in the chart because it could fall into so many categories depending on context. If you are using this terminology with the pupils you can decide which category to put it in. I would put it in the temporal category in the context of these paragraphs.
- *And* is a straightforward additive conjunction adding further information.

Group work

Guided reading and writing: teacher-led tasks

Text level: switching genre
This chapter is an ideal one for repeating the task accompanying Chapter 4, 'No Pockets'. Pupils can inject pace and feeling into their poem.

Independent group work

Word level: prefixes

These tasks have been linked to Chapter 6 but can be adapted to be introduced earlier into the carousel of independent group tasks by removing the sections referring to later chapters.

The tasks look at the prefixes *dis-* and *un-* and the negative tone of words with these prefixes by linking them to meaning and the text. Competent and confident users of the English language play about with the rules once they are learned. Anne Fine uses the word 'unstiffened' in Chapter 6. This may not necessarily be found in a dictionary but describes very well the process of the pupils recovering from their wet playtime. Pupils can go on to play about with prefixes to create words that they might use in their writing. The task is also used to encourage spelling strategies of look, cover and check.

WHICH PREFIX? DIS- OR UN-; UN- OR DIS-?

A Generic
1. Make a chart like the example shown in the supported task listing all the words under prefix as shown or make another selection of dis- and un- words.
2. Only put one or two examples in the remaining columns.
3. Use clear contact and water-soluble pens or ICT to make a reusable resource.
4. Provide extra blank lines so that pupils can skim and scan the book to find their own examples.
5. Pupils, working in pairs, add the right prefix and complete the remainder of the columns, i.e. 'Means', 'Found in Chapter –' , 'About –'.

B Supported
1. Make a chart like the one below and stick it on to card.
2. Provide the headings ('Prefix', 'Means', 'Found in Chapter –', 'About') on a master card.
3. Cut up the chart (possibly leaving 'Found in Chapter –' and 'About' attached to each other). Make it reusable by covering the cards with clear contact and providing water-soluble pens or by placing it on to computer.
4. Pupils work in groups first of all to write the prefix in front of the word and then reassemble the chart.
5. Add extra cards with the headings 'Means' and 'About —' to increase discussion and make the task more challenging.

Prefix	Means	Found in Chapter —	About —
___agreeable	to be unpleasant	1	Bill did not want to be rude to the old lady who helped him across the road.
___tidy	to be messy and leave things everywhere	1	This is what Bill thought of Philip's handwriting. He did not think his was like this.
___willingness	to not want to do something	3	When Mrs Collins tried to take Bill to the chair in the middle of the room, she was surprised when he tried to pull back.
___fairness	somebody feels as though they have been cheated out of something	5	Rohan and Bill for having to write lines after the big fight.
___belief	you just think something must be untrue or unreal	6	Mrs Collins could not believe the sun had waited to the end of dinner time to come out.
___stiffened	feeling relaxed and flexible	6	Everybody started to feel better after their wet dinner time
___steady	a bit wobbly	6	Paul was a bit like this when he ran because he had been ill when he was a baby.
___appeared	to vanish	6	The puddles did this after the sun came out.
___generous	to be mean	6	Bill felt like this after he had beat Paul in the last race.

C Extension

Task 1
1. Learn to spell all the words by look, cover, check.
2. Think of a way of testing a partner's spellings.
3. One of the words in the chart used by Anne Fine in Chapter 6 is quite unusual. Which one is it and why is it unusual?

Task 2
1. Work in pairs and write down the first 10 words that come into your head.
2. Could you put the prefixes *dis-* or *un-* in front of any of them?
3. Could you make words that perhaps you would not find in a dictionary but could use in your writing; for example, decide/undecide?

Chapter 7

A Happy Ending

Characters	Settings	Events	Comments
Bill	Classroom	End of day	
Mrs Collins	Classroom	Expresses concern about Bill being not quite right	
Bill	On the way home	Dispirited	Words relating to moods (p. 91)
Mean Malcolm	On the way home	Whistles at Bill	Bill is angry and describes himself as a person and throws Malcolm off the dustbin
Mrs Simpson	Home	Annoyed at the mess the dress is in	
Bill	Home	Changes his clothes – is a boy again	
Bella the cat	Home	He is the same person	

Whole-class shared text work

Focus areas for discussion

- Reminder of narrative time: it is the end of just one day.
- The incident with Mean Malcolm: why did Bill describe himself as a *person*?
- The chapter title is clear about the ending, but in how many ways could it be *happy*?

Text level: preparation for writing a summary/commentary

The story has already been summarised up to this point, so now there is an ideal opportunity to discuss the gender details in more detail. The chapter is quite a short one to read, and flexible use of the literacy hour should provide enough time for quite a lengthy discussion. I have suggested a pre-prepared list to increase the available discussion time.

The sentence-level work will use the passage where Bill tells Malcolm he is a person. This is quite a nice way of rounding up the discussion. Does Bill indeed find that boys and girls have more in common than he thought?

1. The teacher acting as scribe should prepare on a whiteboard, OHT etc. some of the gender issues raised by Anne Fine. (This is my list and you may wish to change it.) The chapter references are for information only and need not be included:

- Do adults listen as much to girls as to boys? (Chapter 1, crossing the road)
- Are adults as strict with girls as they are with boys? (Chapter 1, late for school; Chapter 5, the fight)
- Do adults expect boys to be a lot stronger than girls? (Chapter 1, carrying the table)
- Do adults allow boys to have more untidy writing because it is thought that they cannot be as neat as girls? (Chapter 1, the handwriting incident)
- Are girls expected to give way to boys in the playground? (Chapter 2)
- Are games in the playground for boys or for girls and never the two will mix?

Is it the same for reading? (Chapter 2; Chapter 5, the comics)
- Do boys behave toward girls in a very different way than toward each other? (Chapter 2, the reluctance to take the ball; Chapters 1 and 7, Mean Malcolm)
- Are girls expected to be generally better behaved and more responsible than boys? (Chapter 3, resisting being taken to the chair to be painted; Chapter 4, the expectation that Bill would do all the jobs he was asked to do; Chapter 5, could a girl in a pink frock really have started a fight?)
- Are girls expected to be more co-operative, while boys are more competitive? (Chapter 6, letting Paul win in the race)
- Clothing issues: Bill is the only person in a pink frock. (Chapter 1, description of clothes of fellow pupils; Chapter 4, no pockets in the dress)
- Do we have boys and girls, or do we have people? (Chapter 7, the incident with Mean Malcolm)

2. Focus the discussion on what Anne Fine was trying to tell the reader about what it is like to be a boy or a girl.
3. The teacher should scribe a paragraph which comments on at least one of the issues raised in the book.

Whole-class work

Sentence level: revising simple, compound and complex sentence structure

Prepare from page 91: 'The frock was a disaster', to page 92: 'I am a *person*.' The passage includes examples of all three sentence types. But, as is often the case, they do not fall neatly into these categories. Older pupils might like to start thinking about the fact that some aspects of grammar are not always governed by hard and fast rules: there can be elements of doubt and discussion.

Pupils should be asked to identify:

- all three sentence types;
- main clauses;
- subordinate clauses;
- connectives.

Simple sentences	Compound sentences	Complex sentences
The frock was a disaster.	He stopped and glowered at Mean Malcolm. Simpson again, he took it so very	(And that is probably why,) when Mean Malcolm whistled at Bill badly.
He shifted uneasily on the lid of his dustbin.		And he strode off towards home, a little more cheerful, leaving Mean Malcolm desperately trying to brush the carrot peelings and tea leaves off his purple studded jacket before his gang came round the corner and saw him.

(pp. 92–3)

These could be placed on cards so that pupils could stand alongside each other to complete the sentences:

Main clauses	Subordinate clauses
he took it so very badly	when Mean Malcolm whistled at Bill Simpson again
(And) he strode off towards home	before his gang came round the corner and saw him

Group work

Guided reading and writing: teacher-led tasks

Text level: writing a commentary

A Generic
1. Pupils may elect to work individually, in pairs, as a sub-group or as an entire group.
2. Pupils select an issue about gender from the shared text session to focus on.
3. The teacher should guide a discussion on which aspect of gender Anne Fine was addressing.
4. The teacher should support the planning, drafting and editing of a commentary on the way Anne Fine addressed the chosen issue.

B Supported
1. Pupils select an issue about gender from the shared text session to focus on.
2. The teacher should guide a discussion on which aspect of gender Anne Fine was addressing.
3. The teacher should support the planning, drafting and editing of a commentary on the way Anne Fine addressed the chosen issue.
4. A writing frame can be provided (see example below):

Chapter and pages	What happened?	What was Anne Fine saying about boys/girls/adults?	Is it true to life?

C Extension
1. Pupils may elect to work individually, in pairs, as a sub-group or as an entire group.
2. Pupils select an issue about gender from the shared text session to focus on.
3. The teacher should guide a discussion on what aspect of gender Anne Fine was addressing.
4. The teacher should support the planning, drafting and editing of a commentary on the way Anne Fine addressed the chosen issue.
5. Pupils should evaluate their commentary on the way Anne Fine approached the chosen issue against their own experience.

Independent group work

Sentence level: conditional forms

'Some weeks later . . .'
This task is linked mainly to Chapter 7 but could be introduced after Chapter 6.

This series of tasks enables pupils to use some conditional forms in the context of thinking about the events in the book through the questions of a reporter. Pupils may find it helpful to do some work based on the chart provided for whole class work on conditionals before going on to construct the answers to the reporter's questions.

A

Some weeks later . . .

Sentence level: if . . . then constructions

Local radio, 8.45 a.m. one Monday morning:

'Following the tale of Bill's strange day as told to us all by Anne Fine, our reporter Sue Quest went to the school to find out more. Unfortunately, as she left the building she dropped her notebook into a very muddy puddle so we cannot bring you her report. But what we can do is send you the questions and part of the answers. We hope some of you listeners out there will get your heads together to finish the answers. Send them back to us and we will pick the one we like best. The winners will spend a day here at your local radio station. There is one rule. You must use one of the following phrases somewhere in your answers:

● could have;   ● might have;   ● should have.'

SUE:	Headmaster, is it true you didn't notice Bill was a girl?
HEADMASTER:	Well, if I knew then what I know now _____
	_____
SUE:	Mrs Collins, how long had Bill been in your class?
MRS COLLINS:	About three months.
SUE:	And one day, he walked into your classroom wearing a pink frock, wearing something even the girls wouldn't
wear, and	you didn't notice anything strange?
MRS COLLINS:	Not at first. If I had looked more carefully _____
	_____
SUE:	Rohan, when Bill tried to join in the football game did you really think he was a girl?
ROHAN:	Well yes, he was wearing that pink frock. I don't know
why,	but I just didn't see Bill.
SUE:	If you could go back to that day, would you do anything differently?
ROHAN:	I'm not sure. Perhaps _____
SUE:	Leila, you let Bill join you and your friends at playtime. Why was that?
LEILA:	Well he just came over looking cold and fed up. We didn't really think about whether he was a boy or girl.
SUE:	And you really didn't realise it was Bill all the time in a pink frock?
LEILA:	I think it was a strange day for all of us. Sometimes, when I think about it I think if only _____
SUE:	Bill, why didn't you let Paul win the race? It had been agreed, hadn't it?
BILL:	I don't know. I just couldn't. I had to win. I suppose it shows that although I was dressed as a girl, I was a girl, inside I
was	still a boy and I behaved like a boy. If I could run the
race	again _____

B

Some weeks later . . .

Choose one of these phrases to put in column 2:

he would have	she would have been	he might have
she might have been	he wouldn't have	Astrid would have been
he couldn't have	he might never have	Astrid might have been
she could have been	he would never have	he could never have

Choose one of these phrases to put in column 3:

had a very different day	very cross	joined the girls in the playground
surprised	very pleased	known what a wumpy choo was
chosen		

Column 1	Column 2	Column 3
If Bill had taken the dress off		
If Bill had said something disagreeable to the old lady		
If the headmaster had chosen some girls		
If Bill wasn't wearing a dress		
If Bill had given the ball back		

C

Some weeks later . . .

The reporter, Sue Quest, decided to go back to the school and do the interviews again. We know what some of the questions were. Can you think of some of the other questions and write the answers? Try to use:

if   then   could have   would have   might have

The questions so far:

- Headmaster, is it true you didn't notice Bill was a girl?
- Mrs Collins, how long had Bill been in your class?
- Rohan, when Bill tried to join in the football game did you really think he was a girl?
- Leila, you let Bill join you and your friends at playtime. Why was that?
- Bill, why didn't you let Paul win the race? It had been agreed, hadn't it?

Now write the new questions and answers.

_____

_____

_____

_____

_____

_____

_____

_____

_____

_____

_____

_____

_____

_____

_____

_____

Plenary sessions

The plenary session enables the teacher to check that the pupils have achieved or are on the way to achieving the learning outcomes of the literacy hour. It may be that it is not appropriate to present some of the group work, if it is going to be used on a carousel basis, although careful timing may ensure that groups who need additional help and support will receive this by seeing how another group has tackled a task.

As plenary sessions are generally short, it is easier to plan for either a teacher-led or a pupil-led plenary rather than try and do both in one session.

Groups who are going to take responsibility for the plenary should be told, at the beginning of the lesson, who they are and what they are going to do. Depending on the task they may wish to choose a spokesperson.

Teacher-led

1. Reviews of what has happened in the book so far.
2. Predictions of what might happen next.
3. Prepare OHTs or flipcharts with examples of pupils' work taken from the guided and independent groups. These can be used to provide feedback in the form of correct and good-quality work and examples of common errors (without naming names). This is extremely useful in providing additional feedback for those who have completed the tasks, and support and guidance for those who are about to do them.
4. Collect examples of poems and paragraphs written by pupils for performance reading exercises.
5. Collect examples of book reviews of other Anne Fine books for discussion (internet bookshops are a good source).
6. Collect related texts to read and discuss.
7. Revision of shared text work and whole class work:

- Why is Bill referred to as 'poppet' or 'dear'?
- Why was Bill's handwriting criticised?
- Simple compound and complex sentences.
- Similes and related vocabulary.
- What might the head have done if he had seen Bill as a boy?
- Revise and extend the *semantic field* of menacing words.
- Reprise the notion of an alternative ending to Chapter 2.
- Revise conditional forms.
- Revise conjunctions.
- Review the meaning and application of proverbs as a means of summarising.
- Sequence a set of events written up as sentences in the wrong order.
- Utilise the use of *upset* and *angry* at the end of Chapter 5 to explore further gender-related words
- Revise the notion of what Anne Fine writes.
- Reading time/narrative time.

Pupil-led

1. Read poems and paragraphs to the whole class.
2. Put forward opinions about toys.
3. Explain the meanings of certain proverbs.
4. Explain how proverbs were matched to extracts.
5. Provide examples of different sentence types from the text.
6. Provide examples of different conjunctions from the text.
7. Provide words and phrases related to time.
8. Provide words and phrases related to the way Bill feels.

Part II

Using Bill's New Frock *beyond the literacy hour*

Extended activities based on specific chapters

The tasks here are listed chapter by chapter, although many of them could be adapted for other chapters. At the end, there are other tasks that cannot be specifically attached to a chapter and relate to the whole book. Tasks have a speaking and listening, reading or writing focus, so that links can be made to the National Curriculum for English. However, in terms of developing the literacy skills of pupils, there will be overlap and integration of these three programmes of study.

The speaking- and listening-focused tasks can be linked to many of the tasks suggested in Part I. Speaking and listening has tended to be the poor relation of the National Curriculum Attainment Targets. However, it is to be hoped that the tasks below will enable pupils to study the book further, and develop the skills of arguing, persuading, listening and discussing.

Some general advice for planning speaking and listening tasks is:

- start off with pupils working in pairs and then move them into fours;
- set time limits for the tasks;
- ensure that there are clear goals to achieve so that the task comes to a discernible end;
- if pupils have to report back to the whole class, ensure that pupils are prepared for this and can choose their spokesperson.

Learning Together Through Talk: Key Stages 1 and 2, is a resource pack edited by Gordon Baddeley (1992) which disseminates the work of the National Oracy Project and will provide further information on ways of managing talk-based lessons.

The writing tasks can also be linked back to many of the tasks suggested in Part I. It is assumed that pupils will have time to plan, draft, revise, proof-read and present, where appropriate. Choices should be made about whether the tasks are suitable for collaborative or individual work. Pupils may benefit from using a combination of approaches. For example, they may have a writing partner with whom they can discuss their plans and first drafts before going on to produce the final version.

Writing frames or guidelines to support many of the writing tasks have been provided, but should only be used if needed. Wherever possible, pupils should generate their own framework for writing.

The literacy hour does not always provide enough time for pupils to spend on the process of writing to produce a piece of writing that is of high quality, is in a style appropriate to its purpose and has a sense of readership. The tasks here are intended to balance the literacy hour tasks.

If pupils are going to use ICT then they should be able to use the computer for the entire writing process, rather than using it to 'type up' a final version.

The reading tasks are intended to allow pupils to study the themes, issues, characters and narrative structure, as set out in the National Curriculum programme of study. In addition, pupils should be able to explore related texts and other books by Anne Fine. There will be very few tasks linked to the book based on prediction, as it is assumed that pupils will have read or heard the whole book and know the story well.

Language studies also feature in this section, as many of the tasks enable pupils to investigate language, language structures and ways of exploring word- and sentence-level work in the context of a whole text.

Summary of tasks

	Speaking & listening	Reading	Writing	Language study
Ch. 1	Why didn't Bill take the frock off?	Compare Rapunzel stories	Bella the cat Mrs Collins's story	
Ch. 2	Playground rules	Following the narrative line	Writing dialogue Bill and Bella	
Ch. 3		Pick a question		Bill and his not quite all pink frock
Ch. 4	Clothes for school			
Ch. 5	Why did the big fight really start?	Cloze procedure Review of comics	Report of the big fight	Synonyms
Ch. 6	Debate	Cohesion		
Ch. 7			Mean Malcolm's story	
Whole book tasks	Simulation	Anne Fine's web of books	Dictogloss Book-making Expectations	Talking punctuation Cohesive ties

Chapter 1: A Really Awful Start

Why didn't Bill take the frock off? (speaking and listening focus)

This task is inspired by a pupil who asked why Bill did not just take the frock off. The obvious answer is that there would have been a very different story. However, much of the Literacy Strategy focuses on pupils understanding the ways in which a narrative is structured and the different turns a plot could take; so to say there would be no story is not a satisfactory answer.

This task enables pupils to explore possibilities and think about cause and effect.

Make a set of cards, giving each card two scenarios/sentences. (If possible use strong card and laminate them.) The game is a version of dominoes, in which the following rules apply:

A/B   Generic/Supported

Pupils should work in groups of 4.

These are the instructions for the task. You could give the groups the written instructions and include reading and following them as part of the task, or demonstrate the task first.

● Put the double card *Bill took off the pink frock and put it in the wardrobe* in the middle.
● Share out the cards face down, three per person.
● Put the remaining cards face down on the table.
● Players can have a turn in one of three ways:
  – put down a card explaining why it fits with the previous one;
  – miss a turn;
  – swap a card with one from the pile on the table.
● If possible the cards should make some sort of sense when read in any direction from the double card, but you might have to settle for just two or three cards in a line making sense.
● The intention is to get all the cards into the game.

Bill took off the pink frock and put it in the wardrobe.	Bill took off the pink frock and put it in the wardrobe.	Bill's mother came back and told him to put it back on.	Bill's father asked him why he wasn't wearing his pink frock.
Bill couldn't find any of his clothes.	He found an old T-shirt that was a bit too small.	He found an old pair of shorts.	None of his clothes seemed to fit.
He put on the old pair of shorts and the T-shirt that was too small.	The T-shirt that was a bit too small ripped under the arm.	At least he still had his trainers and his socks.	He couldn't do the shorts up - there was a button missing.
He crept into his parents' bedroom looking for a safety pin.	He found a button on the floor.	How do you sew on buttons? Bill had no idea.	Bill found a safety pin on his mother's dressing table.
Just as Bill was picking up the safety pin he heard his mother come into the room.	Bill found a needle and cotton in the kitchen drawer.	"What on earth do you think you're doing dressed like that!" said his mother.	Bill climbed out of the window, on to the flat roof of the garage and leapt nimbly to the ground.
"Your mother wants a word with you poppet," said his father.	Bill managed to sew the button on just in time.	Bill ran all the way to school hoping the button wouldn't fall off.	Bill put the safety pin back and told his mother he was not going to wear the pink frock.
I am very disappointed in you," said his mother. "Go back to your room and put that lovely frock back on".	"You seem to have grown a lot lately," said Bill's father. "I think we'll have to get rid of that T-shirt".	Bill's father grabbed the T-shirt, and before Bill could say anything it was pulled off and put in the cleaning rag box.	Bill desperately tucked the pink frock into the shorts. "I suppose it looks a bit like a shirt," he thought.

C Extension

Provide laminated blank cards and water-soluble or dry-wipe pens so that pupils can add their own suggestions.

The task can be used as a precursor to writing alternative directions the story could have taken, with a focus on including 'if . . . then' constructions and other forms of conditional clauses.

Comparing stories: Rapunzel (reading focus)

The version of Rapunzel which appears in Chapter 1 is quite different from some of the published versions that can be found. It is Rapunzel's mother who craves the rapunzel and has to give up her baby to the witch in return for the rapunzel in the witch's garden. Also Rapunzel does make a plan to escape with the prince, although of course it all goes wrong. What might be harder to explain is that when the prince is finally reunited with Rapunzel she has twins, a boy and a girl. If you feel this may take you into territory you do not want to discuss, then ignore this task.

Pupils may be able to discuss why Anne Fine presents Rapunzel as a non-assertive character; and there are a lot of re-written fairy tales where the princess is no longer content to wait for the handsome prince to come along: this might feed the discussion.

Pupils can develop and apply their knowledge of narrative structure, characters, events and settings in the context of an already familiar structure. This is an ideal task for pair work and encourages skimming and scanning.

A/B

Did Rapunzel just wait for the prince?

1. Read about Rapunzel in Chapter 1 of *Bill's New Frock*
2. Find one or two more Rapunzel stories, and write in the table where you found them.
3. Fill in the tables to help you find out how different each story is

All about the characters:

	Character/behaviour of Rapunzel	Character/behaviour of the witch	Character/behaviour of the Prince	Endings
Rapunzel in Chapter 1 of *Bill's New Frock*				
Rapunzel found in _____ _____				
Rapunzel found in _____ _____				

All about the main events and the settings:

	Main events	Where did the main events take place? (settings)	Endings
Rapunzel in Chapter 1 of *Bill's New Frock*			
Rapunzel found in _____ _____			
Rapunzel found in _____ _____			

C

Stories about Rapunzel

	Main characters	Problems	Conflicts	Resolutions
Rapunzel in chapter 1 of *Bill's New Frock*				
Rapunzel found in _____ _____				
Rapunzel found in _____ _____				

(Adapted from Mellor, B. *et al* 1984:32)

Use the table to help you write a summary of what you found out.

_____

_____

_____

_____

_____

_____

_____

_____

_____

_____

Writing from a different perspective: Bella the cat (writing focus)

Bella the cat is the only character in the story who does not see Bill as anything other than himself.

A/C Generic/Extension
Pupils should write a recounting of the series of events as Bill gets ready for school from Bella's perspective, using the first person. They could write it as continuous prose or format it into a cartoon strip.

B Supported
Writing frame:

- I rubbed around Bill's ankles as usual.
- It was just like any other day except that Bill was upset. I wondered why.
- (Bill's) mum and dad were in a hurry as usual.
- When Bill came home at the end of the day he . . .

Mrs Collins's story: looking back (writing focus)

Mrs Collins is vaguely aware that Bill is not quite himself and that he is behaving in a way which she sometimes does not expect. After the day is over she sits and thinks about it.

A/C Generic/Extension
Pupils can write about what Mrs Collins is thinking, but still thinking of Bill *as a girl*. There are some suggestions below of the events Mrs Collins might think about, which can be given to pupils to work from, or the list could be generated as part of the planning as a whole class activity, pair or group work.

The piece of writing could be in the form of a letter to a friend/son/daughter or as a recount.

B Supported
Writing frame:

- When she wasn't chosen to carry the table . . .
- What about that terrible handwriting?
- Fancy talking about Rapunzel like that.
- As for when the class painted her portrait . . .
- I shouldn't have sent her to take back the spare key . . .
- What about that fight!
- She must have felt better when she won the race.

Guidance on the features of a recount and other writing styles can be found in *First Steps Writing Resource Book* (W. Australia Department of Education 1997) and *First Steps NLS Edition: How to Assess Children's Literacy. Literacy Development Continuum* (Pemberton and Davidson 1999).

Chapter 2: The Wumpy Choo

A/B

Playground rules

Plan of the playground

The main playground	grassy area	nursery and infant playground
	Cloakrooms, doors and entry to school	

Playground rules
- Children from the junior classes (key stage 2) cannot go into the nursery and infant (key stage 1) playground.
- No child can go on the grassy area or it will not be grassy for very long.

Unknown to Bill and his classmates, the headmaster had seen everything that playtime. He decided that it was time something was done to change the way the playground was taken over by the boys. He discussed it with the other teachers and they thought of six changes they would like to make.
Of course, there was not enough money to make all the changes so the head asked the pupils to decide.

What would you choose?
- Working together, choose three of the changes below so that both boys and girls have equal use of the playground'. **You cannot change the rule about junior children going into the infant and nursery area.**

Possible changes: (choose 3)
- Cover over part of the playground.
- Buy some wooden picnic tables with benches.
- Cover the grassy area with playsafe tarmac and put up some swings.
- Turn the grassy area into a nature study area with a pond.
- Mark out the playground for games like Hopscotch, and into areas for skipping, marbles etc.
- Put up basketball/netball practice rings.

Draw your changes on the large plan on the next sheet.

Choose someone to explain why you have decided on these changes.

The new playground

nursery and infant playground

Cloakrooms, doors and entry to school

In the A/B task

Pupils are being asked to put themselves in the place of the fictional pupils in the book. An adaptation of the task is for pupils to consider their own playground and any possible changes or modifications.

The emphasis is on discussion, putting forward arguments and supporting them, and listening to other pupils in order to reach a consensus on the new playground. In order to help pupils keep on task, set a time limit for the completion of the task and tell the class that each group must select someone who is going to talk to present their ideas to the whole class.

In addition you could build in *envoying*. This is when one or two pupils (envoys) from each group take their ideas to the next group and ask the next group's opinion on the work so far. This should be strictly timed: so many minutes into the task, so many minutes for discussion. Occasionally envoying involves the envoys going to more than one group (see Baddeley 1992: 17. Baddeley *et al.* 1991: Ch. 5 provides further practical advice on managing group and pair work.)

C Extension

Pupils can undertake a piece of persuasive writing to put forward strong arguments for their choice of changes to be made. Further information about the techniques of persuasive writing can be found in Wing, Jan (1991).

Writing dialogue (writing focus)

A Generic

In Chapter 2, Bill manages to get the football and tells the boys he needs it, but he doesn't say why. Pupils can write a passage which includes Bill, Rohan and Martin as Bill tells them why he wants the ball and what he is going to do with it.

As well as developing the argument and discussion, pupils will have to focus on using capital letters, commas, full stops and speech marks.

Start with: 'The ball happened to bounce . . . moment' on page 29, and add:

'Why?' asked Rohan.
'Because . . .'

Pupils can act out the scene in front of the class or make a tape-recording of it.

Bill and Bella (writing focus)

When Bill got home at the end of that terrible day, the only one he could really talk to was Bella the cat. Perhaps only Bella understood how he really felt at the end of Chapter 2, when he walked away with the 1p chew.

This task, through Bella the cat, encourages pupils to reflect on Bill's feelings and use and apply some of the vocabulary used in the literacy hour sessions.

The box below can help pupils to start to formulate their ideas, but at the same time the restricted space means they will avoid writing more words and phrases than they can work with.

A Generic

> Using the book, your dictionary and your own ideas, write down as many
> words or phrases as you can which describe how Bill felt:

These instructions can be given to pupils to guide them through the planning,
drafting and editing process. This particular set of instructions may help pupils
make connections with other work focusing on conjunctions.

Pupils could make their own prompt cards as follows:

- Put the words and phrases into sentences.
- Read through the sentences, cross out any you don't want.
- Check the sentences you have left.
- Use them to write a piece which tells a reader what Bill told Bella.
- Think about capital letters, full stops, commas and speech marks.
- Think about using conjunctions such as *and*, *but*, *because*, *so*, *then* and so on.

C Extension
An alternative approach is a piece of writing in which Bella narrates how Bill felt at
the end of Chapter 2, her interpretation of events.

Following the narrative line (reading focus)

A Generic
This task lends itself to pair work. It can also be transferred to other chapters or
used with the whole book. (The degree of detail will vary.) Listed below are the
basic instructions to be given to pupils. The supported or extension tasks can be
built in, depending on how far the task is prepared for pupils, by providing the
following options:

> giving instructions only;
> narrative structure on left-hand end of line, no events/characters on the right-
> hand side;
> events and characters provided, no narrative structure on left-hand side;
> parts of each side provided, omitted information listed on the whiteboard if
> necessary;
> draw a thick line down a piece of paper near the middle.

- using the top of the line as the start of the chapter and the bottom of the line as
  the end, write down the main events and the character involved on the right-
  hand side;
- on the left-hand side write in the main aspects of narrative structure:

Setting, Main characters, Problem, Conflict, Complication, Resolution (although
these are usually applied to a whole story they can be applied within chapters
before repeating the exercise with the complete book).

This example is for guidance only:

Narrative structure	Events and people
Setting	Playground
Main characters	Bill, Martin, Leila, Astrid, Flora, Rohan
Problem	Bill heard about Martin's bet.
Complication	The bet was a 'wumpy choo' Bill didn't know what that was.
	Bill took the bet.
	Bill went to borrow a football but got knocked over.
	Bill caught the ball.
Conflict	The boys asked for the ball back. They were angry.
	The boys would not take it, Martin said 'please'.
Resolution	Bill said he would give it back for a wumpy choo.
Problem	Bill discovered what a wumpy choo was and was very miserable.

The National Literacy Strategy training materials have helpful information on narrative structure, as does the *NLS Literacy Development Continuum* in the *First Steps* series (Pemberton and Davidson 1999). In working with chapters in a book you may find that the conflict/complication stages can be in a different order. You can also include a *crisis* element. In any one chapter, or book there can be several problems, conflicts and complications and so the task above may be over-simple. However, it can be a useful introduction to narrative.

Chapter 3: Pink, Pink, Nothing but Pink

Pick a question

A Generic

Listed below are questions about Chapter 3. Pupils can either go through these questions on their own or with a partner, but choose or agree on six to answer. The rest should be crossed out and ignored. If pupils work in pairs there are opportunities to discuss the text and questions, which will address speaking and listening. Included in the selection are questions that deliberately do *not* apply. Identifying these is part of the comprehension process.

This task is easily adaptable to use with a variety of texts.

Note: Pupils are expected to answer the questions as appropriately and economically as possible. Unless you have decided to use the task as a sentence construction exercise, if a one-word answer is appropriate then that is what the pupils should write.

1. How did the children get the classroom ready for art?
2. What happened to the pastels?
3. Why couldn't they use the yellow paint?
4. Why was everyone disgusted with the pink paint?
5. Why didn't Mrs Collins think it was a good idea to paint Bill?
6. Why did Bill pull away from Mrs Collins when she tried to take him over to the chair?
7. What made Bill fall off the chair?
8. How did the glob of pink paint get on to Bill's dress?
9. Why did Mrs Collins give Bill a blue exercise book to hold?
10. While Bill was being painted what did he think about?
11. Was Bill pleased with the portraits?
12. Did Mrs Collins realise how miserable Bill was?

(Adapted from Morgan and Rinvolucri 1983: 13–15)

A/B

Bill and his not quite all pink frock

1. Work with a partner and make sure you read and understand **all** the instructions before you start work.
2. Look at the *adjectives* in the vertical column and the *nouns* in the horizontal column.
3. If you think the words go together, put a ✓ in the right column. For example, the words *pink frock* go together well.
4. If you think the words do not got together well put a x in the right column. For example, the words *fiery fingerprint* do not go together well.
5. Sometimes you might not agree and you will have to discuss and decide whether to put a ✓ or a ✕.

	crayon	paint	picture	frock	hair	slug	finger-print
pink				✓			
brown							
grubby							
muddy							
slimy							
gloomy							
fiery							✕

(Adapted from Gairns and Redman 1986: 37–8)

C

Speedy reading

1. Make sure you read and understand all these instructions before you start work. Discuss them with your partner.
2. See how quickly you can find the adjectives and nouns in the table. (You only need to find *pink* once).
3. Write down the sentence, clause or phrase you have found in the first column of the table below,
4. Look at the next column and write **sentence** or **clause** or **phrase**.
5. Write down the page number from the book in the last column.

I have found . . .	Sentence, clause or phrase?	Page
'*Grubby fingerprints* around the hem;'	Phrase	39

Write your own sentences containing at least one adjective and one noun from the chart.

Chapter 4: No Pockets

Clothes for school (speaking and listening focus)

Bill might have managed to get all the things he was asked to carry safely to Mrs Bandaraina if he could have put something in his pockets – but there weren't any. Most schools have a school uniform, but are they practical?

Children can work with a partner on the following two activities to consider the design of a new school uniform.

A/B

School uniforms for the new millenium

1. Work with a partner and make sure you have read and understood all the instructions before you start.
2. Look at the list of ideas for a school uniform in the chart below.
3. If you want to, you and your partner can add some more in the spaces at the end.
4. Decide with your partner which would be your *number 1,* that is *most important and best idea* for a school uniform.
5. Then find the *second best* idea and mark it *number 2* and so on until you get to the last and least important idea.
6. You might disagree with your partner. Talk about it and try to agree.
7. Work with another pair and look at both your lists. Do you agree or disagree about school uniforms?
8. Who had the best idea of their own?

Ideas for school uniform:	Number
The trousers should be cargo trousers (lots of pockets)	
A choice of trousers, shorts and skirts for girls	
A hard-wearing denim jacket	
A sweatshirt with the school logo on it	
A choice of shirt or T-shirt	
Everything should be the same colour	
The whole uniform should be cheap to buy	
Fabrics should be washable	
There should be a choice of colours but everything should match	
Lots of pockets	
A tie with the school logo on it	
A choice of trousers and shorts for boys	

C

What will the uniform for the millenium look like?

Draw and label a uniform for a boy or for a girl, or a uniform that both boys and girls could wear.

1. Work with your partner and write a short piece about your design.
2. Explain why it is a good uniform for the new millenium.
3. Write your explanation in rough first and show it to some friends to check.

Chapter 5: The Big Fight

Why did the Big Fight really start? (speaking and listening focus)

A lot of the work that pupils do in school is only marked as either right or wrong. When pupils try this task the groups may have different answers (it is not guaranteed); but if they do, an important part of the task is seeing that different answers can still be valued. The basic instructions are listed on the activity sheet overleaf.

The basic instructions are listed on the activity sheet overleaf.

A/B

Why did the Big Fight start?

Work in pairs or groups of four.
1. Make sure you have read and understood all the instructions before you start.
2. Read the list of things that people did in Chapter 5 that led up to the Big Fight.
3. The list is the *order* that things happened in but which was the most *important* in starting the fight?
4. Discuss this with your partner or in your group.
5. When you have agreed fill in the chart using the numbers 1 to 11.
6. Choose someone who can tell the whole class the reason for your answer

Remember! There is no absolutely right or wrong answer.

This is what happened, in the order that it happened:

1. Mrs. Collins gave Bill a copy of *Bunty*.
2. Melissa would not swap her *Beano* with Bill's *Bunty*.
3. Flora had two comics and would not swap one of them with Bill.
4. Rohan would not swap his *Valiant* for Gill's *Bunty* and Martin would not swap his *Victor*.
5. Flora would only swap her *Dandy* 'now or never' even though Bill was getting interested in the *Bunty*.
6. When Bill had got a *Dandy* Rohan tried to make Bill swap it for a *June*.
7. Bill shook his *Dandy* in Rohan's face and Rohan tried to snatch it.
8. Bill was angry when he realised Rohan wanted to give him *June* because of the frock.
9. Rohan tried to take the *Dandy*.
10. Bill Simpson hit Rohan hard on the shoulder
11. Rohan kicked out at Bill and left a mark on the pink frock.

Most important reason		Write the numbers 1–11 in the right space								Least important reason

(Based on *The Theatre Fire* by Harkess & Eastwood 1981: 96/97)

Whole class work:

- The teacher asks each pair/group to present their answer.
- Collate answers on to the whiteboard.
- Have a class discussion about any agreements/disagreements in the answers produced.

C Extension

Pupils can construct their own task as follows:

1. Select a chapter and ask pupils to identify and sequence the main events.
2. Having listed them, pupils can pass them on to another pair/group to go through the same dissuasion process.
3. Pupils can use the discussion and exploration process to support a variety of writing tasks. Examples from Chapter 5:

- What would Mrs Collins tell her husband/son/daughter/friend that evening about the day?
- What would Melissa or Flora or Rohan tell their friends when sending their e-mail messages at home on their computers?
- Write how Rohan felt when he realised Mrs Collins did not believe Bill started the fight.
- Bill realised there was one advantage to wearing a frock. What other advantages might there be?

Review of comics (reading focus)

On the advice of pupils select a range of comics appropriate to the age range of the class. (Read and review them before proceeding with this task.)
If the supply and variety of comics is limited, use the task on a carousel basis, giving each group a different comic to review at the end of the session.

A/B/C
Comics for boys and comics for girls?

1. Work with a partner or in a group and make sure you have read and understood all the instructions.
2. Choose a set of comics to read and review. You do not have to choose the comics in the table. You can cross those titles out and put in your own choice.
3. Use the table below to help review the comics. Do not worry if you cannot write something in every box.
4. When you have finished try to answer the questions on the next page.

Comic	Titles of fictional stories	Titles of non-fiction articles	Other articles	Selection of advertisements	Illustrations and picture
Beano					
Dandy					
Bunty					
June					

The results of our review of comics

1. Is there a comic that you think is mainly for boys?

What is your *evidence* for this?
    stories
    other articles
    pictures and illustrations
    advertisements
    letters

Write your answer here:

2. Is there a comic that you think is mainly for girls?

What is your *evidence* for this?
    stories
    other articles
    pictures and illustrations
    advertisements
    letters

Write your answer here:

3. Is there a comic that you think would be enjoyed by both boys and girls?

What is your *evidence* for this?
    stories
    other articles
    pictures and illustrations
    advertisements
    letters

Write your answer here:

4. Have you noticed anything else about any of the comics that you think is important? (For example some comics may be linked to a TV programme).

Write your answer here:

5. Write a review of one of the comics which can be read to the whole class, or put on the notice-board for everyone to read.

Emotive words (language study focus)

The English language is rich in synonyms, but exercises which ask pupils to identify words with the *same* meaning deny access to the range of connotative meanings attached to words and the effects the words may have in a sentence. Words rarely have exactly the same meaning, and this can contribute to pupils achieving the style and effect they want. Charts such as the one below can be devised quite easily, using a dictionary of synonyms.

A/B Generic/supported

1. Either using the charts below or ones you have devised, delete a selection of words from each column. The more you delete, the harder the task.
2. Pupils fill in the missing words using a range of dictionaries, e.g. thesaurus, dictionary of synonyms.

C Extension

1. Columns for languages other than English could be added.
2. Pupils can explore the context by referring to a text the words have come from.
3. Pupils can explore the meanings and use, through creating a text.
4. Working with the verbs chart may create opportunities to examine time and tense.
5. Working with the adjectives and adverbs chart may provide opportunities to differentiate between these two word classes and their functions in sentences.

Sample charts
(You may not agree with where I have placed the verbs, adjectives and adverbs)

Exploring verbs

Stronger effect	Neutral effect	Weaker effect
Punch	Hit	Strike
Yelp	Yell	Cry
Sham	Pretend	Make-believe
Snarl	Tangle	Interleave
Leap	Spring	Caper
Batter	Hit	Smack
Goad	Egg on	Encourage

Exploring adverbs and adjectives

Stronger effect	Neutral	Weaker effect
Savagely	Fiercely	Dangerously
Serenely	Calmly	Mildly
Beautiful	Pretty	Nice
Frail	Delicate	Flimsy
Colossal	Great	Big
Tremendous	Immense	Great
Abominable	Horrifying	Shocking

Cloze procedure (reading focus)

This task can stand on its own, but would also support the following two tasks. It is similar to the conjunctions cloze procedure task in Part I, in that it is another grammatical cloze.

Use from p. 65: 'Rohan pulled harder', to p.66: 'and it was shocking'. Delete a selection of verbs: *punched*, *yelped*, *thumping*, *pretended*, *kicked*, *tangled*, *leaped*, *hitting*, *egging*.

A Generic

1. Pupils should work in pairs on the text, with the selected verbs deleted.
2. No words should be provided, and pupils should not refer to the original. (If they are really struggling, provide a choice of words, possibly on small cards that can be placed on the extract.)
3. Pupils should agree on a word that fits in terms of meaning and grammatical agreement (i.e. tense, singular or plural and so on).
4. Pupils can compare their own version with the original.

Note: Use this as shared text work in the literacy hour with the text on display and a selection of cards that pupils can pick to fill in a space. They should explain why they have picked their word.

Newspaper report on the big fight (writing focus)

Newspapers in Education provides useful resources to support this, and the previous task. It can be contacted on html://www.nie.northcliffe.co.uk/nie.html or on 01332 332387.

A Generic
Sue Quest reappears (see Part I, p. 45) to interview Rohan and Bill in order to write an article for the local newspaper.
Pupils should devise the questions and write the answers in the way they think the characters would answer them. Possible questions could be:

- How did the fight start?
- Why did you want a boy's comic, Bill?
- Bill, what did you think of *Bunty*?
- Rohan, why did you try to make Bill take *June*?
- What did you think when Bill shook the *Dandy* in your face, Rohan?

Chapter 6: Letting Paul Win

Debate: This class believes that the girls were wrong to try and arrange for Paul to win (speaking and listening focus).

A/B Generic/supported

The girls planned to let Paul win the race and included Bill in their plans. In the end, Bill just had to go on and win the race. He just could not stop himself. The girls were cross at first, and then decided it was for the best because Paul might have realised it was all planned, and he was very happy with being second. Working in pairs/small groups, pupils could complete the chart below, before the debate:

Reasons for letting Paul win	Reasons for letting the race just happen

1. The teacher should select four speakers, two to support the motion and two to speak against it.
2. The selected speakers should have time to prepare their speeches.
3. They can canvass opinion by finding out how groups filled in their chart.
4. The teacher acts as chair; making it clear that there is a time limit on the main speeches.
5. The two speakers supporting the motion should put their case. (This can be done quite flexibly in terms of who speaks, and when.)
6. These speakers can then answer questions from the class.
7. The process is repeated for the speakers against the motion.
8. Further time is available for opinions to be expressed from the class.
9. The teacher takes the vote.

C Extension

Pupils can write a report of the debate, either for a real school newspaper or in the style of a newspaper report.

Further information about report writing can be found in W. Australia Department of Education (1997).

Pupils might like to select a few newspaper stories from the tabloids and the broadsheets in order to compare styles. (See the earlier reference to *Newspapers in Education*.)

Cohesion task (reading focus)

Reference pronouns

When we read a text, particularly a narrative and we come across pronouns, *I*, *she*, *he*, *him*, *they* and so on, we can usually put a name to them. If we cannot it is usually because the author does not want us to, and is creating an air of mystery or suspense. The way that nouns and pronouns are linked through a text crossing sentence, paragraph and chapter boundaries is an example of a *cohesive tie*. Young writers may have difficulties with this. Have you ever read a story written by a young writer, with one or more of the following problems?

● There are so many characters that the reader has lost track of who is who, and the writer probably has too! In other words, the reader does not know who the *he* or *she* referred to actually is.
● Characters or the narrator change throughout from first to third person.
● Characters change sex half way through the story.

Any of these can happen, as the young writer develops the skills of keeping track of characters and events. Tasks like the one outlined below provide a model which helps pupils to see how nouns and pronouns are used in the books they read.

A/B Generic/supported

Select an extract of text which can be placed on one side of A4 paper. Although only an extract, it should be fairly self-contained and complete. (There may also be books you can use, perhaps from Key Stage 1 classrooms, where you can fit a complete story on one side of A4.)

● Pupils should choose a colour for each character.
● Using the appropriate colour, they should map the progress of each character through the extract by joining all the references to that character whether these are nouns or pronouns. (The pronouns can be in any form, personal, possessive etc.).
● This provides a visual map of when characters appear and re-appear. Ask the questions:
　　1. Who is in the extract all the way through?
　　2. Who drops out first?
　　3. Who is mentioned early in the extract and then not again until later?
　　4. How many times is each character referred to by name and by pronoun?
　　5. List the pronouns in the extract.

The extract overleaf gives an idea of how the references to Bill can be joined (adapted from Young 1991: 16–21).

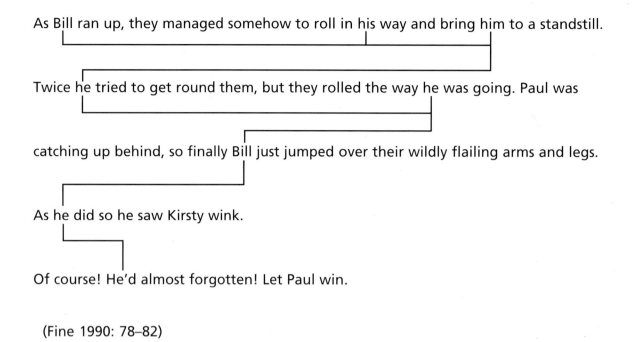

As Bill ran up, they managed somehow to roll in his way and bring him to a standstill.

Twice he tried to get round them, but they rolled the way he was going. Paul was

catching up behind, so finally Bill just jumped over their wildly flailing arms and legs.

As he did so he saw Kirsty wink.

Of course! He'd almost forgotten! Let Paul win.

(Fine 1990: 78–82)

C Extension

Explore and identify different types of pronoun. For example, personal pronouns substitute for nouns:

I, you (singular), *he, she, it, we, you* (plural), *they, one*

The pronouns may occur in different forms according to the function of the word in a sentence:

me, him, her, us, them

them, it, they can refer to non-human but animate characters, such as a rabbit with a name, and to inanimate objects and abstract ideas.

Possessive pronouns can also be included in the chains of reference, for example:

my, your, his, its

For further information on exploring cohesion through texts in the primary school, see Young (1991).

Chapter 7: Happy Ending

Mean Malcolm's story (speaking and listening and writing focus)

We meet Mean Malcolm twice in the story, at the beginning and at the end. What do we know about Malcolm?

- He is part of a gang of boys from the other school.
- He wears a purple studded jacket.
- He's a bit scary. There was a scuffle once when Bill had all the scabs kicked off his ankles.
- He whistles at girls.
- He didn't want his gang to see him after Bill pushed him into the dustbin.

A Generic
Work in pairs to build up a picture of Mean Malcolm. Discuss the questions below:

- How old is he?
- What does he like doing in his spare time?
- What doesn't he like doing in his spare time?
- How does he get on at school?
- What is his family like?
- Does he have any brothers or sisters?
- What are his likes and dislikes in music?
- What are his likes and dislikes in food?

Any other questions about Mean Malcolm?
Write a description of Malcolm.

Working with the whole book

Anne Fine's web of books (reading focus)

There are various ways in which pupils can find out about other books written by Anne Fine:

- they are listed at the front of each book;
- pupils can look in libraries and book shops;
- publishers' catalogues are available.

By far the easiest way for schools on the internet is to access an on-line book shop, for example, www.okukbooks.com/. On these websites you will find the publisher's 'blurb' from the back cover and very often reviews written by children, with opportunities for pupils to submit reviews.

Talking punctuation (language study focus)

A Generic

This task is quite easy to prepare and illustrates the importance of punctuation when reading aloud. It is also quite useful for independent group work in the literacy hour after focusing on punctuation in the whole class teaching sessions. The task can also lead on to pupils acting out a scene for the whole class, or their group:

1. Take a paragraph from the book containing an aspect of punctuation you wish to focus on, e.g. question marks.
2. Provide pupil A with a copy of the paragraph with all or most punctuation removed.
3. Pupil B has a copy of the complete text and must read it to pupil A in such a way that pupil A can add the punctuation to his/her incomplete copy.
4. Both pupils compare and check their versions of the extract.

Book-making (writing focus)

A Generic

One of the most effective ways of providing pupils with a reason for writing and taking their time over the process is to ask them to make a book that will be read to others. The task is for groups of pupils to write a version of the story for younger readers to enjoy.

Planning
- Is the book going to have chapters or not?
- Is it going to have all the events in the original book?
- Is it going to have all the characters?
- Is it going to have new characters?
- Are the characters going to stay the same age?
- Are some of the minor characters going to become more important?
- Are some of the important characters going to become less important?

- Who is going to narrate the story?
- Is the book going to be based on the narrative structure of: setting, problem, conflict, complication, resolution?
- Will the book be more ambitious in terms of narrative structure, e.g. the use of 'flashbacks'?

Format
- Is the book going to be in conventional format?
- If not, will it be, for example, in comic strip form, a pop-up book, a zigzag book?
- If it is comic form, will the characters have speech bubbles?
- Will it need an index?
- Will it need page numbers?

Language
- Will it be in conventional prose style?
- Can it be written in a language other than English or as a dual language text?
- If not, will it be in a form of poetry, for example, rhyming couplets or blank verse?

Illustrations
- Will it be illustrated?
- Where will the illustrations be placed: for example, interrupting the text or on the facing page?
- When will the illustrations be done: when the writing is finished or as it is being done?

Cover and publicity
- What is the title of the book?
- How will the cover be illustrated?
- What 'blurb' will be written on the back?
- How 'authentic' will the cover be; that is, will there be a price and a bar code?

ICT
- Can the book be produced using desktop publishing or a word processing programme?
- Should an accompanying audio-tape be produced?

Reading
- Who is going to read it to another class?
- Will they need practice time on how to read a book to other pupils?
- Could some pupils act out part of their book?

The questions above are guidelines and some pupils may prefer to devise their own schedule of questions or planning schedule which the teacher can discuss with them.

Having thought about these aspects of the book, pupils work through the process of planning, drafting, revising and proof-reading until they can present the finished version. They should keep in mind that the finished book must be of good enough quality to go on the bookshelf, and in terms of content it *must* interest younger pupils.

Writing can be a lengthy process and it is not unusual for pupils to lose heart during the planning and drafting stages. Having decided on the format and shape of the book, it can be very motivating to show pupils a template, so that they can visualise the book as a real entity. Also, arrange a date and time when they can read this book, so that there is a clear goal and deadline.

Dictogloss

This is a task which was developed in Australia for pupils with English as an Additional Language. Pupils have the opportunity to construct a text focusing on grammar, vocabulary, meaning and textual cohesion within the context of a familiar text. The process is as follows:

A/C Generic/extension

1. Tell pupils you are going to read a short text at normal speed and they should just listen.
2. Tell pupils that you are going to read it again at normal speed, and that they can write down five key words (the number of words can vary).
3. Pupils then work in pairs, to pool their key words and reconstruct the text.

B Supported

As the generic version apart from:

1. Provide a list of words and tell pupils to tick five key words as they hear them.
2. Provide a writing frame with six boxes, for example, and key sentences or phrases if necessary.

(Jupp and Harvey 1994: 2–4)

You could initially choose an extract from the book, to enable pupils to become used to the task. They should already be very familiar with the story so they can draw on their memory, as well as on what they hear. However, as a more challenging task, you could use an extract from a related text, or perhaps from *Rapunzel*.

Expectations (writing focus)

This task is intended to enable pupils to study the ways in which boys and girls are presented in the text, and to compare that with their own experiences.

A Generic

Gathering evidence about Bill

Using memory initially, and later research, pupils should note the different ways in which Bill was expected to behave. Pupils are not expected to use all of the following examples, but in pairs or groups it may be possible to collate quite a few on to the whiteboard.

Bill was expected:
    not to argue about wearing the dress;
    to accept being whistled at;
    to need help crossing the road;
    to not *really* be late for school, just need some encouragement;
    to be unable to help carry a table;
    to have very neat handwriting;
    to be pleased to have the star part of reading *Rapunzel*;
    not to question the tasks he was set (*Rapunzel* again);

to keep his dress clean;
to accept that the boys had possession of the playground and girls could not join in;
not to be compliant (when he pulled away from Mrs Collins in Chapter 3);
to do jobs responsibly and willingly;
to read certain types of comics;
not to fight, or start a fight or win a fight;
to co-operate in making someone else feel good (letting Paul win).

Gathering evidence about the girls as a group

The girls were:
willing to let Bill join them and become part of the group;
accepting of the situation in the playground;
able to express their ability to do things like carry tables, kick footballs but did not actively create the opportunities to do so;
expected to get the painting things out;
aware of the needs of others and work co-operatively.

Gathering evidence about the boys as a group

The boys:
took over the playground;
had their own rules which were understood by all;
only applied the rules to other boys.

The task

Pupils should write about the ways in which the author (perhaps) stereotypes boys and girls, and about whether the experiences in the book are similar to, or different from, their own.

If the pupils find it difficult to organise all the information and ideas they have gathered, they can use one of the following writing frames. The first helps mainly with structuring the writing, and the second helps with selecting the content.

B Supported

Writing frame 1: structure

● Write in paragraphs.
● Start each paragraph with your main and most important point.
● Try to group similar and related ideas together.
● Each sentence should make a new point.
● Think about the way you link clauses in your sentences.
● Think about the way you start each sentence.
● Punctuate your sentences correctly.

Writing frame 2: Tabulation and reformation

For further information about tabulation and reformation, see Neate (1992).

The evidence gathering is tabulated under general headings and then written as a piece of continuous prose. This is helpful to pupils who may have difficulty deciding on the focus of each paragraph.

Question	Notes
How was Bill expected to behave differently as a girl?	
How was Bill expected to feel as a girl?	
How do I feel about some of the things that happened to Bill?	
What do I think about the way the girls in the story behaved?	
Did they behave like the girls I know?	
What do I think about the way the boys in the story behaved?	
Did they behave like the boys I know?	

Simulation: a whole-class activity (Speaking and Listening focus)
(The design of this simulation is based on Jones 1985)

Changing the playground: an optional development of the playground task

When a simulation works, it can provide an ideal setting to integrate reading, writing, speaking and listening. A certain amount of reading and a lot of discussion can happen before and during the simulation, and a range of writing tasks can emerge afterwards. Pupils can become very involved in the whole process, and this is the key to its success.

What is a simulation?

Simulations are set up so that adults or pupils can experience a situation as close to reality as the activity will allow. Participants are often given role cards; these are not a guide to acting, but to give the participant a job or a function. Pupils can be themselves (although it has to be said that, as pupils take on the role of adults, a certain amount of acting may be required). Documents can be provided, and these should look as real as possible. Fortunately, computers have made this a lot easier.

The process

- Pupils are introduced to the problem or situation which is the subject of the simulation.
- Pupils are given preparation time, often in groups, where they have a chance to look at documents and think about their role cards.
- The simulation takes place. The simulation must have a controller who can be either in the simulation or outside it. (It can be the class teacher, who may also take on a role.)
- There is a debriefing session at which the participants discuss how things went, either staying in the simulation, or having ended the simulation.
- Some of the role cards or documentation may be rewritten after the first try of a simulation.

The subject of the simulation: the problem

In Part I of the resource pack, it was seen that the head teacher in the story became aware of the problems the girls had in the playground, as Bill won his wumpy choo. He wrote to two playground design companies outlining the problem, provided a plan of the current playground layout and asked for ideas and estimates for a redesigned playground.

One of the companies, Playtime Consultants, made a brief reference to using pupils' ideas in the choice of flowers. The head has decided to expand on that idea and has asked the companies to come and talk to the pupils. One class has been chosen to hear what the companies have to say. They are:

Company 1   Space to Play Ltd
Company 2   Playtime Consultants

Role cards

Simulations should not be stressful, so role cards should be given to pupils who would like to participate. The teacher's knowledge of his/her pupils is very valuable in assigning roles. Although pupils are not expected to act, little snippets of extra information have been included which pupils might like to draw on. Often, when a simulation is well under way and pupils are thoroughly involved, they forget these snippets. This can be a good thing, as it shows they are drawing on their own resources effectively.

Sally Smith, design manager for Space to Play Ltd
Your job is to design playing areas for schools, parks, nurseries and so on. You have been doing this for quite a long time. Most of the play areas you have designed have been very successful, but a few years ago a child had a serious accident in a play area designed by you in a British holiday camp.

B. Jones (male or female), Space to Play Ltd
Your job is to find and buy all the materials needed for the new playgrounds and to work out the costs for new customers. You are very busy with a lot of work to do, but you do your best.

J. Patel (male or female), Space to Play Ltd
You have just joined this company from university. You are Sally Smith's assistant, but would like to have her job one day.

L. Glendower-Newbow (male or female), Playtime Consultants

You started this company a year ago. You used to do all the designing, but because you were so busy you took on a new designer, H. Brook, and he/she designed this playground. However, you haven't much work at the moment and you really need this contract. If you do not get it, you might have to sack H. Brook, but you have not told him/her that (yet).

H. Brook (male or female), Playtime Consultants

You have just joined Playtime Consultants as a designer and this is your first design for an English school playground. You worked in America for a while designing and landscaping gardens. You worked for quite a lot of home owners and worked on all sorts of gardens from very small to very large. You think this is a very good design and that it is a fair price.

F. Bridge (male or female), Playtime Consultants

You are in the sixth form at school and you have been doing a week's work experience with Playtime Consultants. H. Brook asked you lots of questions about your primary school and its playground. You are wondering if this would be a good company to work for when you leave school. *But* what nobody else knows is that you were the child injured in the holiday camp and you know that Sally Smith designed it. You cannot decide whether or not you should say anything.

Miss/Mr/Ms/Dr _____ (head teacher, male or female), _____ School

Note: The class teacher, acting as controller of the simulation, could take on this role as a means of running it.

You really want the school to have a new playground. You have spoken to all the people you need to speak to about permission to do this and the money needed. There is no problem about going ahead with the project but you have only been given £4000. You know that whichever plan is accepted, the school (that is, the children and parents) will have to raise the extra money.

Miss/Mr/Ms/Dr _____ (class teacher, male or female)

You have been working in _____ School for about ten years. You think you are a good teacher, but sometimes would like to feel less tired and less overworked. You are not quite sure about this playground. You can see that there is a problem, but perhaps it could be dealt with by some simple playground rules. And if there is all this money to spend, the school urgently needs new computers.

Other roles
All remaining pupils can basically play themselves.

Preparation
Pupils (and teachers) should be given adequate time to prepare. You should avoid stopping a simulation to clarify something about the process, if possible. It can be very difficult to get back into the simulation if that happens.

Group 1: Space to Play Ltd
The pupils with these role cards should be given time to plan how they are going to present their plans to the school. They should have:

✓ a copy of the letter sent by the head;
✓ a copy of their letter and estimate;
✓ an enlarged plan of the original playground and their proposed playground.

Pupils should also have time to prepare any other documents they think they might need.

Group 2: Playground Consultants
As above.

Group 3: The head teacher and the class teacher
If the real class teacher is taking on the role of the head, the pupil taking the role of the class teacher works alone and then consults other pupils or the real teacher.

The head teacher should think about how to open the meeting and the class teacher should think about how to explain that he/she is not sure about having this new playground and that perhaps computers are more important.

These participants need time to prepare questions to ask the companies and the pupils. They should have copies of all the documents.

Remaining groups
Any pupils without role cards should be grouped together in groups of about four and given time to prepare questions and decide who they are going to question.
   As class teacher, check the questions to avoid overlap or repetition and check that each group knows who is going to ask them.
   Give each group an area to focus on. I have listed some possible areas:

✓ cost of each design and where the money is coming from;
✓ other projects the companies have worked on;
✓ time taken, mess and disruption while the work is being done;
✓ more information about the materials;
✓ other ideas and changes to the plans.

However, if possible encourage pupils to think of their own ideas. Pupils should have as much ownership of the simulation as possible.
   Each group should have copies of all the documents except the enlarged plans.

During the simulation

The controller or the person taking the role of the head must lead the simulation. He/she must introduce and end each stage, and control the questioning. Sometimes the controller will have to make quick decisions about when to end a stage and move on to the next. Keep a certain amount of pace going and try not to let the simulation fade away.
   If the pupils will not be not distracted, you might like to consider videoing the simulation to use in the debriefing stage.

● The head opens the meeting by introducing everybody and explaining what is going to happen; that is, each company will present its plan, then there will be time for questions.
● Company presentations.
● Pupils, head teacher and teacher question the companies: the questioning is managed by the simulation controller.
● The simulation is completed by a vote for one or other (or possibly neither) of the plans.

Debriefing

Use video clips at this stage, if available.

Staying in the simulation
The controller guides a discussion on who made the best presentation and why.

Coming out of the simulation
The teacher guides a discussion on the progress of the simulation, the types of questions asked, how they were answered. Pupils can review their own speaking and listening skills and discuss whether or not they listened, asked good questions, and took turns in the discussion. They may like to consider whether or not their spoken language was appropriate in terms of levels of formality.

Many of these speaking and listening skills can be directly linked to the National Curriculum programme of study. In addition, problems with the design of a simulation often do not emerge until the first run-through.

Adjustments can be made before another class tries out the simulation. I once forgot to give a copy of a letter to a participant that she, in her role, had written. Fortunately, the simulation continued. After some quick thinking, she claimed the letter was a forgery as she had never seen it before!

Cross-curricular links

Mathematics: area, estimating and calculating costs.
Science: strength and safety of materials.
Art: colour combinations and their effects on moods.
Writing: pupil involvement in preparation of documentation, written report of the simulation, rewritten documents and/or instructions, acceptance letter from the head to one company and rejection letter to the other, responses from the companies to the letters.
Reading: use of reference books to find out about materials, colours, design, etc.; critical evaluation of the writing style of the letters from the companies.

Documents
Try to make these look as authentic as possible. There should be nothing unexpected in a simulation which the participants could not cope with. Unless it is essential to the smooth running of the simulation to restrict the distribution of documents, all participants should see them.

Document 1: Letter from head to companies
Format the letter with the name and address of the school, name of the head and address of the companies.

Dear Space to Play Ltd/Playtime Consultants,

It has recently come to my notice that the girls in the junior school cannot find enough space in the playground to play their games. They seem to have no option but to stand around the edge while the boys play a game of football which takes up all the open space.

I enclose a plan of the playground and look forward to receiving your suggestions for changes so that the girls can have an equal share in the space available. I should add that no changes can be made to the nursery and infant playground, which works perfectly well.

Document 2: Letter to head from Space to Play Ltd
Format document by designing headed paper, using addresses, date, phone number, e-mail address, web-site and so on.

To the Headteacher from Space to Play Ltd

We attach a plan of the playground as we see it.

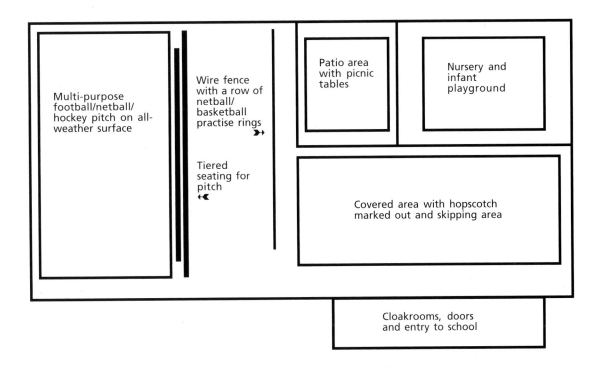

The changes we propose are as follows:

- The football pitch should be clearly marked and also marked as a netball and hockey pitch.
- The pitch should have an all-weather surface for safety and for use in all weather conditions.
- Fixed tiered seating, as well as clearly separating the pitch from the remainder of the playground, will provide ideal audience seating and additional meeting places for pupils.
- Behind the seating, a wire fence with netball/basketball rings will provide a safe practice area.
- The grassy area would be covered with brightly coloured patio paving slabs and picnic tables would be placed on the patio.
- The cover in the covered area would be of the 'carport' type, that is, a flat roof supported on strong posts. This would also provide a lining-up area for pupils suitable for all weathers.
- Games would be marked out on the tarmac under the carport. We suggest hopscotch but we would also like to hear the pupils' ideas.
- We suggest that the covered area and patio area should be used by the nursery and infant pupils at different times from the juniors.
- Total estimated cost: £4300 (not including VAT).

Yours faithfully,

Sally Smith
Design Manager

Document 3: Estimate from Space to Play Ltd
(Format as above.)

Estimated cost of redesign, work and repair for the playground at
_____ School:

	£
Cost of labour and materials is included	
Paint and marking of games pitch	200
All-weather pitch surface	1100
Seating	1300
Fencing, posts and basket ball rings	600
Paving slabs	150
4 wooden picnic tables	150
Covered area structure	800
Total cost, excluding VAT	4300

Document 4: Letter to the head from Playtime Consultants
(Format as above.)

To the Headteacher from Playtime Consultants

We are so glad you contacted us to advise you on the best use of your playground space. We have given your problem a great deal of thought and put our best minds and computers to work on it. We are confident you will be pleased with our suggestions.

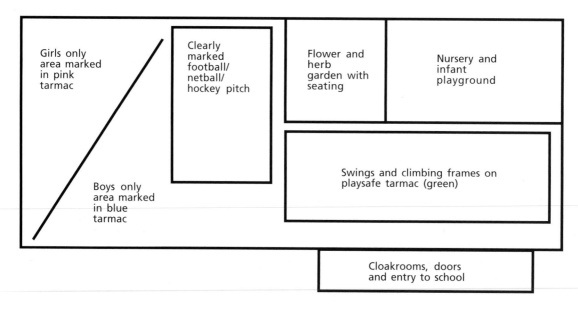

We would like to think that we could design a playground where the space would be available to boys and girls equally. But let's face it, it does not work like that. In our experience, we have found the only thing to do is to provide separate areas for boys and for girls, and the only way to make it work is to colour code the tarmac.

The best way to keep a football game in part of the playground is to mark the pitch. We also suggest all-weather covering.

Children like a quiet area. We suggest that the grassy area becomes a flower and herb garden with seating. We also suggest that the children choose the flowers.

All children like swings and climbing frames. These days it is possible to build very safe climbing frames and to lay a surface which children can fall on to safely. (However, we do suggest you take out additional insurance.)

Total cost : £5450, including labour and VAT. We enclose our easy-to-read, easy-to-understand estimate.

We look forward to hearing from you.

Yours very sincerely,

L. Glendower-Newbow
Managing Director, Playtime Consultants

Document 5: Estimate from Playtime Consultants
(Format as above.)

Estimate for the rejuvenation of the playground at _____ School.
Costs include labour and VAT
We really think you will like this!

	£
Pink and blue tarmac	1000
'Come hail or shine' football/hockey/netball pitch cover	900
Line marking	150
Garden landscaping	500
Garden plants	300
Chill-out seating	600
Swings and climbing frames	1000
'U R SAFE' play area surface	1000
Total	5450

Documents 6, 7 and 8
Enlarged plans of the current and proposed playgrounds.

Cohesive Ties

Lexical cohesion (language focus)

There are several tasks in this resource pack based on *cohesion* (the various ways in which texts are linked across sentences and paragraphs). The task entitled 'Emotive words' (p. 72) helps pupils to explore synonyms, which are forms of lexical cohesion. The task called 'Bill and his not quite all pink frock' (p. 62) draws on synonyms related to the state of Bill's frock. Work linked to Chapter 6 shows how texts are linked to reference pronouns.

This task links with previous ones (in which the progress of Bill's dress is charted as it gets more and more dirty) and looks at synonyms and antonyms. The tasks below will enable pupils to think about the way one word might be more appropriate than another and thus extend their vocabulary. At the same time you can show pupils how some of these words are used and re-used throughout the book, as a form of cohesive tie.

There is also another issue raised by the book. Perhaps we think that at the end of a day at school girls should come home cleaner than boys. Do girls get into more trouble than boys if they come home dirty?

A

Are these synonyms?

Anne Fine uses the words:

dirty
grubby
filthy

to describe the state of Bill's frock.

● Are they synonyms? Do they really mean the same thing?
● Try this sentence:

To start with Bill's frock was just _____ , but by the end of the day it was really _____ .

If the words meant the same thing you could put any word in any space. Were you able to do this?

Are these *antonyms*?

dirty
clean

grubby
spotless

filthy
washed

mucky
immaculate

grimy

unwashed

● Draw a line to join the words which mean the opposite.
● Show your work to a friend.
● Have you joined the same words together?
● If you haven't, why do you think that is?
● Try writing the words you have joined together in a sentence. Use ideas from the book if you can. What about:

At the end of the day Bill's pink frock was filthy but Talilah's bright red satin bloomers were still immaculate.

Bibliography

Books and articles

Baddeley, G. (1992) *Learning Together Through Talk: key stages 1 and 2*, London: Hodder & Stoughton.

Baddeley, G. *et al.* (1991) *Teaching Talking and Learning in KS2*, London: National Curriculum Council.

Benson, G. (ed.) (1995) *does w trouble you?* Harmondsworth, Middx: Puffin Books.

Carter, R. *et al.* (1997) *Working With Texts: a core book for language analysis*, London: Routledge.

Chapman, J. (1983) *Reading Development and Cohesion*, London: Heineman.

Department for Education and Employment (DfEE) (1995) *The National Curriculum for English*, London: HMSO.

Department for Education and Employment (DfEE) (1998) *The National Literacy Strategy*, London: HMSO.

Dixon, P. (1988) *Grow Your Own Poems*, London: Macmillan Education.

Fine, A . (1990) *Bill's New Frock*, London: Mammoth Books; first published London: Methuen Children's Books, 1989.

Gairns, R. and Redman, S. (1986) *Working with Words*, Cambridge: Cambridge University Press.

Harkess, and Eastwood, (1981) *Cue for Communication*, London: Oxford University Press.

Jones, K. (1985) *Designing Your Own Simulations*, London: Methuen.

Jupp, C. and Harvey, A. (1994) 'Dictogloss', *NALDIC News*, no. 3, May.

Leech, G. *et al.* (1982) *English Grammar for Today: a new introduction*, London: Macmillan.

Mellor, B. *et al.* (eds) (1984) *Changing Stories*, London: ILEA English Centre; currently published English and Media Centre/NATE.

Morgan, J. and Rinvolucri, R. (1983) *Once Upon a Time: using stories in the language classroom*, Cambridge: Cambridge University Press.

Neate, B. (1992) *Finding Out about Finding Out: a practical guide to children's information books*, London: Hodder & Stoughton/United Kingdom Reading Association.

Pemberton, L. and Davidson, N. (1999) *First Steps NLS Edition. How to Assess Children's Literacy: Literacy Development Continuum*, GHPD.

Phillips, A. (1998) 'It's just so unfair', *The Times Educational Supplement*, 13 November, 14–15.

Rice, J. (1991) *Bears Don't Like Bananas*, London: Macdonald Young Books.

Styles, M. (ed.) (1986) *You'll Love This Stuff: poems from many cultures*,

Cambridge: Cambridge University Press.

Western Australia, Department of Education (1997) *First Steps Writing Resource Book*.

Willoughby, NSW: Rigby Heinemann.

Wing Jan, Lesley (1991) *Write Ways: modelling writing forms*, Melbourne: Oxford University Press (Australia).

Young, D. (1991) 'Cohesive force', *Literacy & Learning*, No. 6, June 1999, 16–21.

Non-printed media

Fine, Anne, *Bill's New Frock* and *The Country Pancake*, read by Tony Robinson; audiotape pack, Chivers Audio Books, Windsor Bridge Road, Bath BA2 3AX.

http://www.coloacad.org/libraries/adages.html *(proverbs and sayings)*

http://www.nie.northcliffe.co.uk/nie.html *(Newspapers in Education)*

http://www.okukbooks.com/ *(book reviews)*

A glossary of terms used in the National Literacy Strategy can be found on: http://www.standards.dfee-gov.uk/glossary